STAND

SILENT

STAND

SILENT

By

HOWARD PETERSON

To Al
Good Luck

Howard Peterson

VANTAGE PRESS

New York   Washington   Atlanta   Hollywood

FIRST EDITION

Copyright ©1975 by Howard Peterson

Published by Vantage Press, Inc.
516 West 34th Street, New York, New York 10001

Manufactured in The United States of America
Standard Book Number 533-01352-6

CONTENTS

STAND

SILENT

MEDALS ARE FOR HEROES

According to those ancient sages, a hero, more often than not, is born either of desperation, determination, or both. A hero is any person who has the strength of mind and spirit to encounter danger with firmness, fortitude and courage. Webster defines gallantry as conspicuous bravery or courage, with mettle, spirit and an almost gay indifference to danger or hardships. It is distinguished from heroism which is superlative courage in fulfilling a superhuman purpose against odds, while valor implies illustrious bravery, fearlessness and audacity, especially in fighting. Should a person in uniform possess any of these qualities the chances are excellent that they may become eligible to receive a decoration.

A decoration is a nation's grateful acknowledgment of fidelity in an individual. A decoration is conferred upon an individual for a specific act of gallantry in action. On 7 August 1782, George Washington first established honors for the American soldier: "... ever so desirous to cherish a virtuous ambition in soldiers, as well as to foster and encourage every species of military merit, directs, that whenever singularly meritorious action is performed, the author shall be permitted to wear upon his facings, over his left breast, the figure of a heart in purple cloth or silk, edged with narrow lace or bindings. Not only instances of unusual gallantry, but also of extraordinary fidelity and essential service, in any way, shall meet with due reward."

To honor the 193 heroes who survived the ill-fated

1

Charge of the Light Brigade on 25 October 1854, at Balaclava, the Victoria Cross, Great Britain's highest military decoration, was created. The plain but prized decoration was, at first, cast from the metal of Russian cannon captured at Sebastopol. In June of 1857, at Hyde Park, a young Queen Victoria pinned the Cross on five survivors of Balaclava, chosen by lot to represent the five regiments that had charged "half a league into the Valley of Death." The Charge of the Light Brigade saw men rise to heights that since that time has stood as the definition of courage for all men in all nations.

When the United States created our highest military decoration, the Medal of Honor, the firm requirements for its award were modeled on those of the Victoria Cross. With few exceptions, decorations are always of a distinctive design, while a medal is almost always in the form of a disk. The Medal of Honor, America's highest award for gallantry in action is not a medal at all; it is a decoration. Rarely is it ever awarded by the Congress of the United States, although on certain occasions it is. Whenever possible it is presented by the President of the United States. At present, it is the only decoration awarded to American men in uniform which is worn about the neck—although this was not always so. The first Medals were pinned on the tunic of the recipient.

By resolution of Congress, 12 July 1862, to be presented ". . . in the name of the Congress of the United States, to such non-commissioned officers and privates as shall most distinguish themselves by their gallantry in action and other soldierlike qualities." On 3 March 1863, the Medal was made available to commissioned officers with "gallantry in action" the only qualification. Thus did the first Medal of Honor (1862-1896) become applicable to all men in uniform.

The first Medal of Honor was designed by Anthony C. Paquet. The obverse of the decoration, set on a five-pointed star which was tipped with trefoils, contained a crown of laurel and oak in the middle of thirty-four stars, the number of states in 1862. Minerva, personifying the United States, stands with left hand resting on a fasces containing a shield blazoned with

2

the arms of the United States while she repulses Discord, represented by snakes, with the right hand. All of this suspended by a trophy of crossed cannons, balls, swords and the American eagle. The clasp contained two cornucopias and arms of the United States.

On 30 September 1905, by an executive order, President Theodore Roosevelt proclaimed that the presentation of a Medal of Honor would always be made ". . . with formal and impressive ceremonial and the recipient would, whenever possible, be ordered to Washington and the presentation be made by the President."

The first Medal of Honor to be earned was for an action which took place on 13-14 February 1861, when Assistant Surgeon, United States Army, Bernard John Dowling Irwin, at Apache Pass, Arizona, "Voluntarily took command of troops and attacked and defeated hostile Indians he met on his way." The first recipients of a Medal of Honor were members of the Mitchell Raid during the Civil War.

It is most properly called the Medal of Honor. Recent legislation has been enacted to refer to it as the Comgressional Medal of Honor.

SOLDIERS OF THE PLAINS

Back of every conflict between the white man and the Indian was the white man's fear and natural distrust of all Indians, or a treaty that took away the Indians' land and made them live where they did not want to live.

The American Indian was a fierce and willing fighter who jealously guarded his territory from invasion. The American Indian placed an extremely high value on any piece of ground he called home. This so-called home consisted of any land that was cut by his ponies' hooves. In his struggles against the white man, Indian treachery reached its zenith and more often than not bordered on cowardice. With sneaky wiles and sly tricks, the Indian attempted to overcome the great advantages conceded to the white man.

To the Indian, the white man seemed possessed by an all-consuming greed for land. With this unclaimed virgin territory stretched out before him, the white man reached out his hand to take it. The Indian could not understand why anyone would build a fence around a piece of land already considered free and then say it was his. Although some whites considered this land fit only to raise Indians and, while they continually hoped for a crop failure, the majority were indifferent.

In the death struggles that followed, the old primitive ways of the Indian were doomed to defeat. The red man did not give up without a terrific fight however. He fought a heroic, often spectacular, inevitably futile war for the possession of his ancient lands. Bitter animosities, engendered by generations of inter-tribal feuds, prevented the many Indian tribes of the American West from uniting in defending their homelands against the white intruders.

Accustomed as they were to the wild excitement of the chase, the Indian believed that to kill was noble and to labor degrading. The Indian was incapable of understanding warfare as the white man fought it. He saw it only as the killing of people or the running off of pony herds. He hunted man the same as he hunted other game. He was highly skilled in concealing his own movements. As a horseman he had no peers. His fleet, tough little ponies gave him mobility. He usually evaded conflict, save under conditions which appeared most favorable to him.

In the leaders of the warring Indian tribes, the American trooper encountered stubborn, intelligent men, who were not impressed by the white man's military reputations and who refused to fight by white man's rules. When impatient, cocky young men, fresh from the East, and eager to earn a reputation for themselves, underestimated the leadership and fighting qualities of the illiterate Indian, they not only invited disaster upon themselves, but most often paid for their mistakes with their lives.

THAT THIN BLUE LINE

The annals of our Western yesteryear are stuffed to overflowing with story after story about famous and brave men. Yet buried deep within the musty files of the United States War Department, recorded in the cold official vernacular of the military, are the fantastic stories of some of the Old West's greatest heroes. Here can be found some of the most stirring episodes in American history. The symbols of our Army's faith have always been honor and tradition, loyalty and duty, by deeds and not by words, with the flag waving over some obscure frontier post, the guidon snapping in the rush of the charge, the bugle calls floating on the still air to stir the fighting heart.

The Army post was usually located out on the plains where it baked in the broiling hot sun, or was perched on some barren, brown hillside. It was quite often stockaded, always ugly and drab, its shape seldom varied and it had a dusty parade ground. The trooper had to fight the Indian, the heat, blizzards, the bottle, each other and boredom. When he rode his horse he did so ever so warily, for this was hostile territory.

The West was a great natural arena in which was fought a bloody series of conflicts. The East pitied the plight of the poor red men and cursed the army as a gang of cutthroats. The poor trooper was damned when he did and damned when he didn't. The trooper usually found himself outnumbered in some minor skirmish which meant life or death to him.

7

After years of frustration, years spent in chasing an elusive foe, the most successful formula for defeating the crafty redman proved to be a surprise attack at dawn when he was less alert, or during those cold winter months when the Indian was wont to lay dormant and his superior horsemanship was of no distinct advantage to him. The Indian's immobilization could be further hastened by running off, capturing, or destroying his large pony herds. The confiscation and destruction of his supplies, which he had usually obtained only after great difficulty, also tended to dampen his fiery fighting spirit. The tactic of running off the enemy's pony herd was nothing new to the American Indian. In fact, it was an ancient Indian ruse adopted by the trooper and used quite successfully by him against the Indian.

To be a good Indian fighter, the trooper had to possess several outstanding qualities. He had to guard his ever-so-meager physical strength so that it not be wasted without effort. He must never allow himself to be out-generaled and he must never waste his skimpy supply of ammunition. Under no circumstances must he allow himself to become separated from his command, and above all, he must never allow himself to be taken prisoner by the Indians. Before this should happen, there was only one recourse left. He must have nerves of steel, to think and act independently when the occasion arose, yet preserve military cohesion by obeying the commands of his superior officers according to military tactics. He had to be an excellent shot, for he usually carried his entire supply of ammunition on his person.

The scene of a conflict might change from one point to another with great rapidity due to the extreme mobility of the Indian, so the trooper was engaged in many running fights, most with obscure names and scant details. The "yellowlegs" might have to ride hard or the "walk-a-heaps" march vigorously to pursue and overtake the fleeting Indian in order to engage him in open battle. When this happened the trooper almost always found himself at a great disadvantage. Once the fleeing Indian had allowed himself to be overtaken, he was

8

ready to fight and had, by then, chosen a strong defensive position. After marching long distances and undergoing great hardships, the trooper would usually arrive at the scene of battle in an extremely exhausted condition. He was usually in a greatly reduced condition of strength due to the lack of sufficient food and rest.

The trooper could not prepare to do battle with the Indian in advance. He had to be in readiness at a moment's notice to fight the wily savage after their own particular mode of warfare, on their ground and at their time. And when at times, it became necessary to engage the Indian in hand-to-hand combat, it had to be done without a moment's hesitation or command.

To see these soldiers on the plains in hostile Indian territory after protracted marches, wearied and reduced by exposure and insufficient food, at first glance would be marked down as slouchy soldiers. Compared to the gayly bedizened and dashing French Hussar, or the precise and machine-like German Uhlan, or the prim and straitlaced Britisher, one would most certainly be correct. But in the American trooper was something seen in no other army in the world.

For when the bugle sounded, these apparently ungraceful soldiers would move with a motion that dazzled the eye. It was owing to these qualifications that we had such excellent Indian fighters. In this elegant soldierly grace were the finest fighting men in the world. The American soldier does not have to be driven to his duty, only led, and on those occasions when it was necessary for him to assume command, he did so without question. Here are forgotten investments in courage, blood and self-sacrifice. Deeds of personal heroism and individual courage were called forth.

Most of the details surrounding the American trooper seem to be half-fact, half-fiction. But because bullets are non-selective, because they faced death in the performance of their duty, because there just never seemed to be enough troops to go around, those that were available were scattered about the Indian frontiers in a parsimonious manner. The trooper, well-

9

disciplined, well-organized, and with those inner flames called morale and *esprit de corps,* was a better fighting man than the Indian.

Most assuredly acts of heroism and gallantry in action are not confined strictly to those in uniform. This is by no means an attempt to slight those brave soldiers and civilians who fought at places like Adobe Walls, Beecher's Island, the Wagon-Box Corral or the Hayfield fight. Nor to those brave souls who fought at other such obscure places as Crazy Woman's Fork or Chugwater Creek. Nor to all of the other unpublicized and seemingly unimportant battles, big or small, where brave men's deeds went unrewarded. To all of those unheralded heroes who guarded and protected our wilderness frontiers, if there be any glory in fighting, let it rest on men like these. They possessed a quality which, for want of a better word, is called valor.

The following is a partial list of the 419 men who were awarded 422 Medals of Honor during the Indian campaigns from 25 March 1865, to 30 December 1891, save Surgeon Irwin and Private Oscar Burkhard. This was the Army of our Western frontiers. For sheer bone and grit, match it if you can.

A CAPTAIN OF THE STRONG

Even the least knowledgeable of civilian laymen has very little trouble understanding the strategy and tactics of a close-knit pitched battle where the number of troops engaged is large, the casualties heavy and the results decisive.

However, few non-professionals can even begin to appreciate, let alone try to understand, a completely unheralded campaign composed of little more than a dogged, wearying, ruthless pursuit, carried on by a small, poorly equipped army of highly resolute and determined men, chasing yet even a smaller body of highly mobile hostiles, perhaps capturing here and there a little worn out band, disabling a few once in a while, and maybe now and then killing some diehards, until at last, the enemy, beaten, run to earth like an animal who wouldn't give up, reduced by exposure and exhaustion, now only a mere pittance of their original strength, with all recourse in search of succor expended, surrenders. There seems to be absolutely nothing good that the uniformed critic can consider glorious or spectacular about what has transpired, although the soldier had faced many hardships and death. Those objectors, originally opposed to such actions begin to cast unwarranted aspersions against the lowly soldier, and they start to wonder why it took him so long to accomplish such a seemingly simple end to an unjust struggle.

In such an awesome and unglamorous undertaking as has just been mentioned above, the risk of life and limb of the

11

troops in the field who were doing the actual fighting were usually far greater than it is in what we today like to refer to as conventional warfare. For it was here, along those wild, virgin and untamed frontiers, in some of the most rugged, remote and God-forsaken areas on the surface of the earth, that the savage enemy, almost without exception, subjected those poor unfortunate soldiers who were unlucky enough to fall into their hands alive, whether already suffering from grievous battle wound or not, to the most horrible, hideous and unbelievable tortures that the human mind could possibly conjure up in a hundred years. But the poor soldier, who, the critic feels, only has one duty—to obey the orders of his superior officers—comes in for much unmerited censure from the same group whose minds think evil thoughts while their mouths speak many bitter untruths of the soldiers' conduct during those trying times. Especially do those critics respond ever so loudly with oratory, if to them, for no apparent or sound reason, a trooper becomes enraged beyond reason by the untold suffering or the unspeakable torture of a "bunkie." Then this temporarily maddened soldier forgets himself and allows his emotions to override his civilized morals and he begins to sink to the ugly level of his savage foeman in the inhumane and barbaric treatment of his captured enemy. It is, therefore, to the utmost and eternal honor of the American soldier that such incidents are noticeably few and most certainly, even for those few, no one condones or justifies such conduct, but few there are who try to understand such actions.

That ever so small army in blue, which was left scattered parsimoniously throughout those isolated sections of the great American West, as a result of the stringent manpower commitments of the Civil War in the East, had more than proved itself capable of some of the hardest and most desperate of campaigning against the savage and wily Indians of the American West.

As events were later to bring to light, this constituted as dangerous and difficult a duty as any army in the world has ever found it necessary to undertake. Because, for one thing, there was such an abundance of campaigning, and there most certainly was more than enough to go around so that no man need feel that he had been slighted of his share in any way. It abounded with many and varied, sometimes thrilling, and yet again too often, tragic incidents. Volume upon volume has already been written about the heart-rending suffering, the plain and simple romance of those "good old" and glamorous days of yesteryear, which, without reservation, makes for interesting and exciting reading today. It is an acknowledged fact that few men, if any, of those gallant and intrepid soldiers who actually saw service of one kind or another west of the Mississippi River, from 1865 to 1890, did not more than once place his life in peril, in many ways, in perhaps at least a score or more of bloody battles and deadly engagements or, in many a long and hard, but now forgotten campaign. Such dangerous and bitter, yet determined campaigning would, of a certainty, require talents of the highest order.

Now if there ever should be any single individual who, by his indomitable resolve, his persistent devotion to duty and his unrelenting self-sacrifice chosen as a typical representative of the knightly American soldier, let that one person be, with no reservations, one Guy V. Henry, the almost unchallanged leader of courageous men, and honor member of the bravest of the brave.

Guy Henry was born the son of a military family at Fort Smith, in the Indian Territory. He graduated from West Point in 1861, a mere slip of a lad. He was to remain slight of built all of his natural life, but as the following events were to prove, a man's stature has little or no bearing on any particular given situation, when resolutely backed up by a courageous and determined will. In four years of bloody fighting, while engaged in some of the most sanguinary conflicts of the Civil War, from the outset at Bull Run to Cold Harbor, Guy Henry was three times mentioned in dispatches and five times was he breveted for his conspicuous and extraordinary gallantry in action. He was to emerge from the bitter fighting with the brevet rank of a brigadier. By the time he had managed to attain the ripe old age of twenty-three, in the early throes of the struggle, his dash, daring and resolute leadership, his thoughtful and considerate compassion for human life, his feeling and understanding concerning the problems and comforts for the troops entrusted to his command, had merited for him an appointment as a Colonel of the Fortieth Massachusetts Volunteers.

So then it came to pass on 1 June 1864, at Cold Harbor, Virginia, for heroic and successful fighting when he "led the assaults of his brigade upon the enemy's works, where he had two horses shot under him," Guy Henry was to receive the highest distinction which can be bestowed upon a soldier, the awarding of a Medal of Honor.

With the cessation of hostilities in the east, which had seen brother pitted against brother, Guy Henry was reassigned to the Third Cavalry Regiment, which was at that time, garrisoned along the wild and untamed Western frontiers. Many of the old line field officers found it extremely difficult to adjust to the reduced rank of a subaltern, but Henry accepted his new duties with a cheerful relish. His new assignment placed him first in Arizona, where he was arrayed against the bloodthirsty and white-man-hating Apache. It was here, for better than two years, that he commanded a battalion of cavalry, which found itself engaged in some very very hard scouting.

Following Custer's "famed" expedition into the Black Hills of the Dakota Territory in 1874, the winter of that same year found Guy Henry stationed at Fort Robinson, which was also located in the Black Hills of Dakota Territory.

The day after Christmas, Henry was ordered to take a small detail of men into the Bad Lands to evict some errant gold miners who had been plying their trade in defiance of treaty stipulations. With enough rations and forage to last a full thirty days, the small body of men sallied forth from the gates of Fort Robinson, headed for the Bad Lands some three-hundred miles distant.

The weather, which had been unimaginably severe, even for this place and at this time of the year, saw the temperatures

14

varying little from minus twenty degrees below zero to minus forty degrees below zero.

Their *journada* was to prove to be fruitless, however, as no miners could be located. On their return trek to Fort Robinson, the entire command, both men and animals alike, which had already suffered the most terrible of hardships from the cold, was overtaken and fallen upon by a Plains blizzard.

Now the "Eastern city tenderfoot," who might not be altogether familiar with such a weather manifestation as a Plains blizzard, should imagine if he can, the fiercest of all gales, spawned in the frozen Arctic northlands, filled with a multitude of tiny, icy needles, each of which is capable of drawing warm blood as they seek out and locate the tiniest patch of exposed flesh. Paint a mental picture in the mind's eye, of an endless, rolling country, completely devoid of a shelter of any kind, such as a copse of trees or a deep gully, with a driving, blinding sheet of snow pushed violently onward by the biting wind, with the temperatures ranging somewhere in the neighborhood of fifty degrees below zero. Then you will have a vague idea of just what terrors an average Plains blizzard can hold.

It was none not too unlike that by which the command suddenly found itself completely surrounded. The storm engulfing the tiny band, shortly after they had broken camp on what they had hoped was to be the last day of their return journey, became so intense that it was, at once, deemed much safer to walk than to try and ride the horses. Any thoughts they may have entertained of returning to their campsite of the night before was completely out of the question. To keep moving forward was the only sensible thing to be done. The troops dismounted their faithful steeds and began a desperate struggle over and through a deep, unyielding blanket of white.

Before much time had elapsed, many of the men began to sink to their knees, exhausted. They were physically helped into their saddles by Henry's own hands. But a blizzard of such magnitude as this one grants no man quarter, so that finally, it swarmed upon and overwhelmed the entire party,

15

weakening it further and to such an extent that it soon arrived to a point where it seemed almost impossible to proceed further. But in an organized sort of desperation, the horses were remounted and urged forward with little knowledge as to exactly where they were. Unable to see more than a few feet in any direction, trusting fully to the natural instinct of their mounts, they pushed frantically, inexorably onward, Henry in the van. Men struggled mightily to keep ice-incrusted eyelids from closing over eyes already swollen and reddened from lack of sufficient rest. Sleep was utterly out of the question, for to close one's eyes to sleep was to invite sure death.

Then, just when it seemed as though the small knot of brave men were doomed to perish in the elements in this white wasteland, they happened upon a solitary ranch, located in the lee of a small hill. As soon as the animals had been cared for, the men crowded into the tiny ranch house to begin the slow and agonizing process of thawing out frozen limbs and digits.

Everyone was in a bad way of some sort, as none of them had escaped the numbing effects of the frigid temperatures. The men's faces were red and flushed from the terrible beating of the merciless wind. Their eyes were puffed and red from lack of rest and closed to mere slits from the constant squinting in an attempt to reduce the glare. They moved about in the slow, half-dead shuffle of a zombie.

The next day, after the storm had subsided somewhat, the men made the return trip to Fort Robinson. They were in a deplorable state, broken in health, spirits as a low point from the icy cold they had been forced to endure.

Henry's face was so black and swollen that, when he met his wife, she was unable to recognize him. Henry's gloves had to be slit into strips to remove them from his puffed hands and each strip of glove brought with it a hunk of raw, bleeding flesh as it was pulled free. All of his fingers were frozen to the second joint and the flesh had already sloughed off in several places exposing white bone. One of his fingers was later amputated and until the day he died, Henry was unable to close his left hand completely. Yet Henry, accepting such pain and

16

misfortune as a part of a good soldier's lot, uttered not a single whimper. Being naturally thin, Henry suffered much greater from the ordeal.

Every one of the men was to later swear that had it not been for Henry's indomitable persistence to keep them awake and moving, and not allowing them to succumb to the cold, the entire command would surely have frozen to death that terrible day.

Yet all of this pain and suffering was to seem minor compared to what Henry was asked to endure some two years later. With the Custer debacle just days away. Henry now found himself with General George Crook along the Rosebud River in command of the left flank of the left wing of Crook's army, located in a tiny ravine and, to all practical intents and purposes, completely surrounded by hard-riding, quick-shooting Sioux and Cheyenne Indians who surely out numbered them at least five to one. The rest of Crook's strong force was, at that time, too heavily engaged with other savage foemen to offer Henry and his beleaguered men aid. The Indians relentlessly delivered bloody attack after bloody attack, upon Henry's troops, all of whom had dismounted and deployed in line, save the field officers.

Henry, to show his contempt for the shooting qualities of the Indians, and to keep panic from seeping into the men, rode defiantly back and forth in front of his own hastily constructed breastworks, steadying the men, exhorting them to take aim and fire slowly, picking targets so as not to expend their meager supply of ammunition. Now he led a vigorous charge which relieved the pressure on another besieged and greatly imperiled troop.

Then, as the battle continued to range unabated, it was, during one of the many wild and reckless charges by the Indians, that Henry was horribly wounded in the face. An errant Indian rifle ball struck him just under the left eye, passed completely through the upper portion of his mouth and nose and emerged below the right eye. The shock of the speeding missile was like the blow from a sledgehammer. Henry's face

17

was instantly smeared with a red gore and his mouth became filled with blood.

But a man of Henry's fighting spirit would not allow such a thing to cause him to become unseated in front of the men, although he did sway ever so slightly in the saddle. He continued to remain upright, all the while valiantly, urgently, mightily, striving to rally the men for a charge.

But even a man of Henry's self-determination could not overcome the inevitable effects of such a wound. His mind no longer able to bear the excruciating pain took over and he slumped unconscious, plummeting heavily to the earth. It seemed at this moment as though fate were about to deal Henry a fatal blow. At the exact second he was tumbling from his horse, the war-painted savages delivered a vicious onslaught against the not-too-tenable left flank of the line.

The troops, momentarily leaderless, though fighting tenaciously, gave ground grudgingly to such an extent the Indians were able to pass over Henry's prostrate form. Fortunately for him he was not struck by any of the flashing Indian ponies' hooves as they thundered about him. The men of Henry's beloved Third quickly rallied to stem the onrushing Indians and succeeded in forcing them back, reoccupying the ground they had been forced to vacate just moments before.

And a good thing it was for Henry, at least before any of the Indians succeeded in collecting his scalp.

Henry was gently lifted and ever so tenderly assisted upon his horse and then helped to the rear for medical assistance.

Unable to speak above a faint croaking whisper, unable to see even the slightest, scarcely able to hear and each and every breath coming with the utmost of difficulty, Henry mumbled to the doctor. ''Fix me up so I can go back.''

His wound was dressed temporarily, as best they could with what meager medicines were available. But time could not be spared to linger. All through the long, agonizing hours of daylight, while the battle raged furiously about him, flaring into one long, thunderous cacophony of sound, then ebbing momentarily, only to flare once again, Henry lay on the hard bare ground. No one could be spared from the battle line to ease his pain, and he endured his sufferings in silence.

The weather during the daytime was fearfully hot and Henry became consumed with thirst, but there was little water, and no shelter from the burning sun. During one brief lull in the fighting, a trooper passed the helpless man lying on the ground, and paused compassionately to offer aid, by brushing away a swarm of large, blue and bloated flies from Henry's bandaged and blood encrusted face.

In a terrible-sounding, pain-racked gurgle, spewed through fearfully swollen and bleeding lips, Henry managed to murmur, "That's all right, soldier. It's what we're here for."

Executing a steady, organized and fighting withdrawal, the heavily besieged left flank of the line managed to effect a confluence with the main body of troops and the Indians, unable to withstand determined resistance, quickly departed the field of battle.

The first order of business, without undue hesitation, was time given to consider the plight of the sorely wounded. The means of offering them comfort and solace were of the slenderest. The column had divested itself of all but the barest of necessities to give it mobility against the Indians. The nights, as always, became uncomfortably cold.

All through the darkened hours, Henry lay shivering, listening to the men excavating a final resting place for those brave souls who had fallen during the days hard fighting, wondering perhaps if one of the graves might be his.

The next day, a pair of sturdy saplings was cut from the river's edge, trimmed and placed between two army mules, travois-fashion. An army blanket was tightly lashed between the two poles and on it Henry was gingerly placed. He would be forced to make the entire two-hundred-mile trip to Fort Fetterman in this most uncomfortable fashion.

The travois was, of necessity, short, and several times during the early going Henry's head was bumped by the rear mule, each blow causing almost unbearable pain to Henry's countenance. At last, someone suggested that perhaps they should turn the poor man about. This procedure mercifully ended the blows to Henry's mutilated face, but placed him in such a position over the foremost mule's hooves, that he was subject to being kicked to death at any moment. At one point during the long journey, one of the mules stumbled and fell, dashing Henry to the hard ground where he struck his head.

While the others stood aghast, Henry, with an unbelievable iron self-control, made not a sound of complaint. Henry's only food during the entire horrendous trek was a broth made from what birds could be shot by the men.

Finally after what seemed an eternity, the somber cortege neared Fort Fetterman. One last obstacle lay in their path and it was to force yet another unmitigated mishap upon the gallant officer. The river, usually crossed by means of a ferryboat, which was moved from shore to shore by a series of ropes and tackles, was running high and swift.

As Henry was being prepared to be moved across the river, the ropes controlling the ferry parted and the swift current made quick work of the ferryboat against some unusually large rocks, leaving Henry within sight of, but beyond reach of, comforts and medical attention.

Some of the rough and tough old campaigners turned their faces hastily away, swiping at a moisture which had suddenly gathered in their eyes, but Henry, true to his colors, remained silent.

An offer was made to transport the sorely stricken officer across the raging torrent in a small skiff, if he were willing to take the risk. Should trouble beset them in mid-stream and the skiff were to overturn, Henry would, in all probability, be drowned. With two men to handled the paddles and another brother officer to cradle Henry in his arms, the trip was made successfully.

Henry's wife had been waiting for him at Fort D.A. Russell, some three-hundred miles away. At first, she had heard that her husband's wound had been fatal, but later, a reassuring letter from him, long before he reached Fort Fetterman, made her determined to join her husband there.

The railroad extended only as far as Medicine Bow. Beyond there was little more than one-hundred miles of unsettled wilderness. Even though she was with child, time after time, Mrs. Henry attempted to join her husband, but on each occasion was forbidden to go forward as safe passage beyond could not be guaranteed.

Finally, when an escort for Henry himself could be spared, he was sent from Fort Fetterman to Fort D. A. Russell. During a stop-over at Medicine Bow so that the 4th of July could be celebrated, as he lay pain-racked on his cot, two recklessly fired bullets passed through the tent where he lay and missed his head by scant inches.

Next day, as the train was passing through Sherman, the altitude, coupled with the medicines he had been administered to relieve the pain, weakened his heart action to a point where he hovered on the brink of death once more.

Since he had been wounded, Henry had thought only of his anguished wife. Upon arriving at Fort D. A. Russell, he refused to get into an ambulance, wishing to spare his wife the sight of him in such a deplorable condition. Supported on either side and with a superhuman resolution to convince his wife he was not seriously injured, Henry walked to the door of his quarters.

Mrs. Henry had been instructed to control herself as she stood waiting in the doorway.

After a quiet greeting, Henry was laid on a sofa. The bandages were gently lifted from his mangled features so that he might have one single glance at his wife, then the bandages were tenderly replaced.

Mrs. Henry, unable to bear her grief any longer, rushed from the room and broke down completely into uncontrollable, convulsive sobbing.

Everyone expected Henry to die, but die he would not. With his frail physique, he struggled pitifully, but his indomitable will to live overshadowed all else. He lost the sight of one eye permanently.

The following year found him in the saddle in still

21

another campaign with Crook, where, on one particularly warm day, he fainted and fell from the saddle. Insisting that they place him in the shade of a nearby tree, he bade them continue, firmly informing them he would rejoin the command come evening when the weather had cooled. And what he said he would do, he did. He was ordered to return to camp, but managed to avoid this through a technicality, staying in the field for six more weeks, until finally, weakened and nearly spent, he was transported home bodily, still protesting vehemently.

Thirteen years later, Henry was commanding the Ninth Cavalry at Fort McKinney, Dakota Territory. The Ghost Dances of the Sioux brought additional troops to the Pine Ridge Agency. That particular saga of Guy V. Henry is yet another story of bravery in which he was to earn the brevet of Major-General, bringing his total of brevets to six. He was later to serve during the Spanish-American War, with distinction until his health disintegrated completely and he collapsed.

At no time would Henry request relief from his duty, saying, "Here I was sent, and here I will stay until my duty is done."

He died as a soldier should die, in harness, so to speak, his duty complete, his heroic achievements being the inspiration for those who were to follow. He was laid to rest with perhaps just such an epitaph as "Here Lies An American Soldier, A Captain Of The Strong."

A PROFESSION OF ARMS

History has committed to parchment no more dramatic conflicts that those which were fought between the nomadic redman and the blue-clad army, on the plains, in the deserts and in the moutains of the American West. Apache Pass, Arizona, had been for many many months, like an open festering sore. Then, for some unexplained reason, Cochise decided to let the wound heal and live in peace with the white man, for the time being anyway. Mail coaches once again were allowed to pick their perilous journey through Apache Pass unmolested. Although, at times, when an infrequent raid did occur, as long as no whites were killed, it was attributed to roving hands of renegade Apaches.

Then one day toward the end of the year 1860, a terrible seed was sown which, when it germinated and grew, brought a horrible and tragic, savage and brutal war to Apache Pass country, stretching unspeakable atrocities over many long and agonizing years. A band of marauding Apaches had raided a small ranch about twelve miles from Fort Buchanan, driven off some cattle and presumedly carried off a small boy. As soon as the news of this new Indian depredation reached the commandant of Fort Buchanan, he promptly dispatched sixty men to search for the boy and cattle. In charge of the detail was an inexperienced Lieutenant George Bascom.

Apache Pass cuts through the heart of the Chiricahua Mountains. About halfway up the uneven slope of the pass was a stone relay station used by the coaches. Several of Cochise's people had contracted to supply the stage station with wood. These Apaches, with their families, were camped about six-hundred yards from the station near a small spring. Lieut. Bascom knew of the Indians camped near the station, knew them to be peaceful Indians, but nevertheless made a beeline in that direction, feeling this was an excellent place to start his search.

When the troops arrived at the station, Cochise, accompanied by several members of his family, appeared to inquire about the presence of the soldiers in the area.

Lieut. Bascom immediately opened the conversation by ordering Cochise to return the missing child, to surrender the stolen cattle, or face military punishment if he did not comply. Lieut. Bascom was cocky, short-tempered and his inexperience with the Indians caused him to become furious at Cochise and his slow ways. Then, Lieut. Bascom made a fatal move.

He ordered the Indians arrested until they returned the missing child and the stolen property.

Cochise, seeing that his pleas of innocence were falling upon deaf ears, let out a blood-curdling warwhoop and leaped for freedom. Cochise's sudden and totally unexpected actions caught the troopers by surprise.

They fired a futile volley at the disappearing chieftain and then seized five of the Indian braves and imprisoned them.

Cochise, seething with rage at the trick played upon him, had his warriors quickly surround the soldiers and they opened fire at once. The Indians' fire grew steadily more intense. Several of the troopers were hit. That night, one of the soldiers volunteered to attempt a daring trip for help.

The next day, Cochise once more appeared, waving a white flag.

Lieut. Bascom, two soldiers and three members of the stage station crew, who considered themselves friends of Cochise, sallied forth to converse with the Apache chieftain. The white men soon discovered that Cochise was attempting to perpetrate a trick, which would take them captive. Lieut. Bascom and the two soldiers were lucky, for they managed to extricate themselves from the Indian trap in time, but not so fortunate were the three station employees. But unknown to Lieut. Bascom and the beleaguered men of his command, help was on the way. The soldier who had gallantly volunteered to go for help, made the trip safely and reported Lieut. Bascom's dilemma to the officer commanding. A party of fourteen picked infantrymen was quickly assembled, mounted on mules and hastily dispatched. Knowing that Lieut. Bascom must, in all probability, have wounded men among his command in need of medical assistance, Captain and Surgeon Bernard John Dowling Irwin volunteered to lead the rescue detail. They set out on the evening of February 13th in the midst of a heavy snowfall.

By the morning of February 14th, the intrepid little band of rescuers had covered the ensuing twelve miles under the most trying of conditions and had now reached the long, winding canyon leading to the plateau, where Lieut. Bascom and his men lay besieged. As the rescue party attempted to approach the pass, a band of howling, screeching Apaches blocked their path with the intent of punishing Lieut. Bascom further for his rash actions.

Urged on by the thought of the wounded men of Lieut. Bascom's command, Capt. Irwin began to issue orders, intent upon reaching the men who might require his services.

"Right-into-line, all-right-men, look-smart-now, extended-order, steady-men, carbines-at-the-ready, prepare-to-charge, bugler-sound-the charge."

Whooping and hollering, the men surged forward, urging their lop-eared chargers onward. Now, Capt. Irwin was no line officer, but his orders and methods proved to be textbook perfect. The Indians gave way and Capt. Irwin had won the day.

The next day, as the soldiers slowly withdrew from Apache Pass, they noticed a large flock of buzzards circling overhead, a short distance away. As the men approached the area which had attracted the loathsome birds, they came upon the dead bodies of the three employees, horribly tortured, before merciful death and then unspeakable mutilations performed after death.

Capt. Irwin immediately decided on an eye-for-an-eye and ordered summary executions, at once. The captive Indians were taken to a nearby copse of trees and there hung on the spot, the worst death possible to an Apache.

GAUNTLET OF FIRE

From Valley Forge to Viet Nam, there have always been Americans who thought that duty, honor and love of country were words worth fighting for when the chips were down. This is the tradition of heroism, gallantry, dedication and self-sacrifice by our men in uniform.

In all probability, very few people have ever heard of Little Coon Creek, Kansas. Probably fewer still have ever heard of Company A, Third United States Infantry Regiment.

In the month of September 1868, Bucks County, Pennsylvania born Corporal Leander Herron was acting as a dispatch rider out of Fort Dodge, Kansas.

Due to the manpower commitments of the Union in the East during the Civil War, the army in the West had been greatly depleted, which necessitated a falling-back from the frontier. This allowed the various Indian tribes of the Great Plains to ride about freely, virtually at will, to plunder and murder white settlers with a wild, savage and ruthless abandon.

Because of the alarming increase in Indian depredations, the stage line was compelled to discontinue its erratic service along the Santa Fe Trail. The army was forced to carry its own dispatches—kind of like the Pony Express. Roving bands of Indian warriors forced these army dispatch riders to travel mostly during the hours of darkness for their own safety and to avoid detection. There was a small sod-fort establishment at Big Coon Creek, about forty horse miles east of Fort Dodge,

27

which served as a relay station for the dispatch riders. The little sod-fort was garrisoned by a sergeant and ten enlisted men.

As the month of September approached, the nights in Kansas became quite chilly and the soldiers garrisoned at Fort Coon had to depend quite heavily upon dried buffalo chips for fuel. In a relatively short period of time, most of the chips nearest the fort were used up, so that the soldiers had to venture further and further from the scant protection of the little sod-fort in their relentless quest for more and more chips. Seldom in these perilous *journadas* did the men fail to encounter savage warriors in various-sized bands lying in wait for them behind some hillock, copse of trees or hidden in some arroyo.

Consequently, as the events began to unfold for the battle of Little Coon Creek, a wagonload of firewood was quartermastered from Fort Dodge to Fort Coon, thereby raising the curtain on the first act of the fight.

Corporal Herron, acting as a dipatch rider, first met the mule team and government wagon loaded with firewood as he was returning from Fort Larned to Fort Dodge with mail and dispatches during the darkened hours of September 1st. The wagonload of firewood was, at that time, proceeding stealthily toward Fort Coon in the bright moonlight. The wood detail consisted of four enlisted men.

The next day, September 2nd, as the curtain went up on the second act of the fight at Little Coon Creek, Corporal Herron was called into the office of his commanding officer and given some important army dispatches. He was told that the papers would have to be carried during daylight hours because of their importance and, also, Corporal Herron was the only experienced dispatch rider available and therefore he would have to travel with no sleep. At the same time he was warned that Indian smoke signals had been observed to the east of, and in close proximity to, Fort Dodge along the route Corporal Herron was soon to ride.

After he had eaten his morning chow and the red ball of fire that was the sun had taken the morning chill from the air, Corporal Herron, accompanied by Private Paddy Boyle, departed the gates of Fort Dodge on swift Army mounts headed in the direction of Fort Coon, their first relay stop, and the Indian smoke signals.

After they had ridden about thirty nerve-racking miles out of Fort Dodge, without any serious incidents occurring, yet imagining Indians behind every hill and bush, Corporal Herron and Private Boyle began to enter the tortuously twisting and turning ravines of Little Coon Creek. Because they had had to travel slowly and with extreme caution, Corporal Herron and Private Boyle had quickly consumed the hours of daylight. As they began to enter the ravines of Little Coon Creek, the sun had disappeared beyond the horizon and the moon began to shed its dim glow on the ominous looking surrounding terrain, cloaking everything and casting eerie-like shadows.

Suddenly and without any warning, nerves taut, eyes red and swollen, ears straining to the limit, Herron and Boyle could distinguish quite clearly the dull booming roar of Army carbine fire mixed with the sharp, high-pitched slap of pistol fire, intermingled with savage yelling, thundering hooves and screaming horses, all caught up into one long continuous cacophony of sound. Quickly dismounting their horses and holding the animals' nostrils to prevent their whinny from alerting the Indians of their presence in the area, the two battle-wise troopers moved forward along the sandy creek floor. Thus did the third and final curtain go up for the fight at the Little Coon Creek.

The two men warily approached the din and clamor, squinting and straining their eyes to try and see through the seemingly impenetrable darkness. As they slowly and cautiously rounded a particularly sharp bend of a ravine, they could barely distinguish, in the murky dim moonlight, that a large band of hostile Indians had apparently surrounded and laid siege to a small wagon train.

As the two troopers watched from the fog-like gloom, the Indians made what appeared to be yet another concerted attack upon the beleaguered wagon train. However, the tiny force presented such a withering volume of gunfire that serious

29

enough casualties were inflicted upon the Indians to cause them to beat a hasty retreat beyond the range of the deadly maelstrom of lead. Herron and Boyle looked at each other and without a word being exchanged between them, each man knew exactly what had to be done.

Remounting and prodding their startled horses into a full gallop, Herron and Boyle dashed headlong into the fray, hollering and firing their service revolvers right and left with telling effect. As they burst through the line of surrounding warriors, they saw that instead of a wagon train, the Indians had nearly encircled the wood wagon and the four troopers who had manned it.

The Indians now made yet another sanguinary attack which, with the help of Corporal Herron and Private Boyle, was also beaten back.

Taking stock of their perilous situation, it was quickly decided that someone would have to ride for help fast, lest they all die on this God-forsaken spot of Kansas prairie.

Paddy Boyle immediately volunteered to give it a try. Without a further word or hesitation, Private Boyle leaped aboard his mount and made a bold and daring dash through the Indians for help from Fort Dodge.

The remaining trapped men stood and waited in silent prayer until they heard several rapidly fired shots in the distant stillness of the night and could only assume that Boyle had failed in his rescue mission. The men's shoulders sagged with fatigue and despair. All hope of remaining alive now seemed lost.

Looking about, Cp. Herron realized that a better defensive position had to be found if they were going to continue to resist the Indians. The wagon detail had been using the old wood wagon as a barricade for their defense, but now the Indians were beginning to tighten their surrounding circle, making the troopers' position even more untenable.

A short distance away, to their left and to their rear, was a small, deep buffalo wallow. So while the Indian warriors were busily engaged in regrouping for yet another assault on the makeshift fort, the soldiers, some with what appeared to be grievous wounds, exerting seemingly superhuman effort and cursing like the troopers they were, managed to push, pull and slide the old wood wagon, so that it acted as a covering over the buffalo wallow. This placed the troopers in a much better and more secure position in which to defend themselves.

All through the seemingly endless long hours of the night, this small band of intrepid, brave, weary, wounded, thirsty, tired and hungry men continued to reach into their ever-dwindling supply of ammunition and repelled attack after attack upon their own particular spot of hallowed ground. No man was exempt from doing his part in holding off the Indian attacks. If a man was too severely wounded to maintain his post with a rifle, he sat and loaded weapons for those fit to shoot. Unattended wounds became encrusted with blood and dirt. Pain was born without a whimper.

However, even though they continued to resist in a most exemplary manner, they all knew that none of them would live to see the next sunrise, barring some sort of a miracle.

Dead Kiowas began to pile up around the buffalo wallow-old wood wagon fort. After each Indian attack had been beaten back, the bodies of the slain Indian warriors were just a little closer to the desperate men. In a few short minutes it would be dawn, and with it the possible end of a gallant struggle.

Cpl. Herron saw the Indians massing for still another and with all probability, the final attack. Taking stock of their ammunition stores, the unwavering band of determined men found themselves down to a total of twelve rounds, all told. Passing around a plug of tobacco, each man bit off a generous chaw, settled himself down to wait, swearing to sell their lives as dearly as possible.

Suddenly Cpt. Herron saw a group of horsemen ride slowly out of the nearest arroyo. Cpl. Herron raised his carbine and drew a bead on one of the dark outlines. Each of the others sighted in on a shadow and waited. Sensing something was amiss, Cpl. Herron called for one of the group to step forward and be recognized, feeling that it might be some sort of Indian trick.

With a hearty hail, Paddy Boyle urged his horse forward and cautioned Herron not to shoot. Then the whole detail advanced. It was a unit of the 7th Cavalry From Fort Dodge. The Kiowas were fast disappearing over a hill in the distance.

Paddy Boyle had been pursued by four Indian warriors for almost thirty miles, right up to the gates of the fort, but he made it.

The wounded were taken back to Fort Dodge where they all made rapid recoveries from their wounds. Cpl. Herron and Pvt. Boyle continued about their delayed business of delivering dispatches. When the old wood wagon was hauled back to Fort Dodge, it resembled an oversized prickly pear tree. Dozens of arrows protruded from it at every conceivable angle. Upon taking count, it was discovered that the old wood wagon contained more than 500 arrow and bullet holes.

Cpl. Herron was not asked to volunteer, but ran this gauntlet of Indian fire by his own choosing. Charging into that vortex of Indian fire took raw, vital courage. Cpl. Herron's citation for the Medal of Honor reads as follows, "While detailed as a mail carrier from the fort, voluntarily went to the assistance of a party of four enlisted men who were attacked by about 50 Indians at some distance from the fort, and remained with them until the party was relieved."

To those who might be curious as to why Pvt. Paddy Boyle did not receive the Medal of Honor was because of one of the ambiguities of the time concerning the award of the Medal. In the days of yesteryear, the person receiving the Medal had to request it. (It has since been changed.) Evidently Pvt. Boyle did not consider his achievements either heroic or gallant.

HEROES ALL

"Sandy" Forsyth had gone and gotten himself in one hell of a fix somewhere on the Arickaree Fork of the Republican River in eastern Colorado in the fall of 1868. The sagas of Scouts Trudeau and Stillwell, sent for help by Forsyth, is a legend in itself. Upon the scouts' arrival at Fort Wallace, Kansas, Captain Louis H. Carpenter, with troop H of the Tenth Cavalry, was ordered to hasten to the rescue of Forsyth.

Carpenter and Forsyth, being long-time bosom friends, saw Carpenter well on his way during the early morning hours of 23 September 1868. The pace was a fast one. Carpenter had issued orders that if any of the mule teams pulling the supply wagons gave out, they were to be shot and the wagons abandoned. By nightfall they had advanced some forty miles. As soon as the sky turned gray in the east the next morning, Carpenter and his men were under way. Once again they traveled well over forty miles before halting for a rest.

Early the following morning, two more messengers from Forsyth's command came into view. Taking thirty of the best mounted troopers, Carpenter set out in the direction he assumed Forsyth to be. The messengers were only general in direction and detail and Carpenter had no maps of the area. After traveling about eighteen miles and it still being early in the day, as they topped a spur of land which afforded Carpenter a view of the surrounding terrain for miles, he saw to his right a broad valley through which meandered a narrow silver streak. In the center of this valley, in the center of this silver streak, was an island. From that island, rose a solitary cottonwood tree. Carpenter ordered the horses put into a dead run as they galloped down the valley toward the island. Galloping across the river bed, the first to enter the rifle pits was Carpenter. The cavalry had arrived in the nick of time.

Captain Carpenter had performed a very commendable feat in his march of over one-hundred miles to the relief of Forsyth. The battle he was to fight three weeks later was one of the prettiest in execution of all those during the Indian campaigns.

Captain Carpenter had returned from the rescue of Forsyth on October 1st. By October 10th, he was on the march once again and hot on the trail of some Indians who were leading him toward Beaver Creek. On October 12th, he reached the Beaver, about one in the afternoon, where the troops went into bivouac.

The next day they followed the Beaver south, covering about thirty miles. Once more the troops encamped for the night. All of the next day they continued their march down the Beaver, keeping on the lookout for Indians. That night, it was decided to begin the return trip the following morning.

At about seven A.M. the next day, October 15th, the troops were ordered to saddle up. Because the south side of Beaver Creek was hilly and difficult to traverse and offered many opportunities for ambuscades, the column was ordered to move to the north side of Beaver Creek, which was comparatively open. A detail was sent to dig down the side of the creek bank to facilitate the speedy movement of the wagons. The detail had hardly ridden a thousand yards when a band of Indians dashed over a hill to their rear with the intention of cutting them off from the main column. The Indians were almost upon the detail before they were noticed. Captain Carpenter quickly sent a thirty-man detachment from the main column to assist in the retreat of the detail.

Now it became the Indians' turn to be threatened to be cut

34

off from the rear. The Indians quickly withdrew before they became imperiled.

Captain Carpenter immediately realized this small band of savages, in all probability, were a part of a larger party, so he forestalled any pursuit and fell slowly back to camp. The wagons at once forded the creek, the men dismounted and deployed as riflemen to cover the retreat of the remainder of the column. As these troops prepared to cross the creek, it was noted that a large increase in Indians had appeared on their flanks and rear. The troops fell back slowly toward the creek until they came under the protective fire of the dismounted riflemen, and then crossed the creek.

Captain Carpenter immediately had the wagons placed in a double column, with H Troop on the flanks and in the advance, deployed in open order. Troop I covered the rear. With these arrangements being completed, the column began to move slowly and steadily along the creek bottom. As soon as the column began to move, a large body of Indians made an appearance and charged, taking every advantage of ravines, trees and bluffs located on the south bank of the creek. Realizing their position on the creek bottom was extremely untenable under such conditions, Captain Carpenter ordered the wagons to move to higher ground, all the while continuing to drive off the Indians without hindering the progress of the column.

At one point, they encountered a deep ravine in which some Indians had secreted themselves. Having no doubts about the ravine for what it was Captain Carpenter ordered a detail to charge the ravine, into which the detail poured several volleys of carbine fire at close range. This action caused the Indians to exercise more caution in the future in attempting to occupy ground with insufficient strength of warriors.

About one P.M. in the afternoon, the Indians gave an indication of breaking off the fighting, but half an hour later, they once more appeared at the rear of the column. On and on they came, until it was estimated that upwards of six-hundred warriors were present. Emboldened by their numbers, the Indians rushed the column from all quarters. Things took on serious tones.

Captain Carpenter realized the march could not be continued and still repel such a force, so he quickly looked around and selected a place to make a stand.

A short distance to the front was a small knoll, from which the ground fell away in every direction. The troops, remaining well disciplined, reached the knoll, where the wagons were at once corralled. In less than two minutes the Indians were upon them in all their savage fury. The troopers' well-timed, well-aimed volley took a tremendous toll of savages. When finally the attack was driven back, dead Indian bodies lay within fifty feet of the wagons.

Because the weather was warm, because the men had by now been engaged for almost eight hours, a move was made for water to relieve both men and animals. Once more the wagons moved out in double column, headed for the Beaver. The Indians, having lost stomach to face disciplined fire, withdrew. The column reached the Beaver with no further incident.

The losses suffered by the Indians in this fight, plus those suffered at the hands of Forsyth at Beecher's Island, had a profound sobering effect upon the Indians.

The troopers obeying Captain Carpenter faithfully escaped with a few men wounded, some seriously, but none killed. Captain Carpenter's tactics throughout had been most admirable. He was breveted for the fifth time and awarded a Medal of Honor for the relief of Forsyth and the Beaver Creek affair. Well did he deserve them both.

"Was gallant and meritorious throughout the campaigns especially in the combat of October 9-15 and in the forced march on September 23, 24 and 25 to the relief of Colonel Forsyth's Scouts, who were known to be in danger of annihilation by a largely superior force of Indians, " reads his official citation.

THE MEANING OF COURAGE

Webster defines courage as being the attitude or response of facing and dealing with anything recognized as dangerous, difficult, or painful, instead of withdrawing from it.

By the time 1870 had rolled around, Nebraska had already achieved statehood and law and order had been established to a small degree. It was now possible for a person to move about without each and every movement being done at the risk of life and limb.

Most of the Indians had either settled peacefully onto reservations, or moved deep within the formidable and foreboding Black Hills of Dakota Territory. Even Red Cloud, the great Sioux war chief, seemed willing to live in peace with the white man, for the time being at least. However, small bands of marauding Indians still continued to plague the white settlers and keep this wild and untamed frontier in an uneasy state.

May 15th dawned bright and clear for Irish-born Sergeant Patrick Leonard. Sgt. Leonard was called to Post Headquarters and given an order by his commanding officer to lead a detachment of four troopers on what appeared to Sgt. Leonard to be a purely routine assignment. Sgt. Leonard and his detail were instructed to search out certain specific and troubled areas, in an attempt to locate several head of cattle that were reported to have strayed from the small farms located near the army post. Before their day was done and the sun had set, before their mission had ended, the entire detail of five troopers would have earned for themselves the Medal of Honor.

As dawn was releasing the first glow of morning and the crows flew away, cawing rustily in the frost-tinged air, the men were up and preparing to move out. As the sun converted itself into a red ball of fire hanging in the sky, and began winning its battle with the chill morning air, Sgt. Leonard, accompanied by Pvts. Canfield, Hubbard, Thompson and Himmelsback, all from Troop C, 2nd United States Cavalry, departed the gates of Fort Hartsuff at a slow trot, happy to receive a break in the otherwise dull routine of garrison duty.

Sgt. Leonard first led his small detail on a foray to a little brook called Spring Creek, hardly more than a stone's throw from the Little Blue, and not too distant from the place where missing cattle had been located in the past. Although it was still early in the morning, by the time the troopers had reached Spring Creek, the sun was warming the day quite rapidly, so as they swung tired legs clear of cantles the troopers dismounted to slake their thirst in the cool, crystal clear waters of Spring Creek.

As the ever alert sergeant knelt to fill his canteen with the icy water of the creek, he noticed a thick, black pall of smoke on the horizon. More than mere chimney smoke from some farmhouse stove was this, and its size indicated urgency. Quickly alerting the other troopers of the detail, Sgt. Leonard and his men hurriedly remounted their startled horses. Jabbing the mounts with blunted cavalry spurs, the animals were prodded into a full gallop, and the small force of troopers went thundering across the prairie in the directin of the smoke column with a cloud of dust flying from pounding steel-shod hooves.

As they drew nearer to the column of smoke, it became obvious that a farmhouse was burning. Farmhouses burned fast in this neck of the woods and by the time the troopers arrived at the farmyard, the fire had almost burned itself out, having consumed all of the combustible material it could reach. All that remained was a pile of black, smouldering ash. The area surrounding the burned-out farmhouse was littered with a conglomerate of debris that evidently, at one time, had been the contents of someone's home. Close to the well, where the soil was damp, one of the troopers found hoofmarks made by Indian ponies.

They told an old and familiar story. SIOUX!

A thorough search of the outbuildings and pastures confirmed the area devoid of any livestock. The troopers made a quick search of the immediate area and could turn up no bodies. This could mean but one thing. It appeared as though the occupants of the farmhouse had been taken captive and carried off by the Indians to suffer untold tortures before they were mercifully murdered by their captors. Without a moment's hesitation, as visions of past white captives flashed before their eyes, all five troopers knew exactly what their duty must be. Without a word of command or a glance at each other, each trooper vaulted into his saddle, ready for action, even that which might cost them their lives.

The trail left by the red hellions was clear and easy to follow. The renegades, flushed with an easy victory and much plunder, undoubtedly did not expect such a quick pursuit.

Sgt. Leonard guessed that a fair-sized party of about thirty bucks had probably gone loco on fire-water and jumped the reservation, looking for more white man's whiskey. They would have to be halted quickly lest more stolen whiskey resulted in much more serious consequences.

The little band of intrepid men seemed to give little thought to the fact that should they overtake their prey, and Sgt. Leonard's estimate was correct, they would, in all probability, be outnumbered by odds of at least five to one.

Concern for the safety of any white prisoners compelled the troopers to lash their mounts into a full gallop, heading north along the plain Indian trail, which led toward a fairly large and thick copse of trees. Thundering across the prairie at full gallop, it did not take the pursuers long to overtake the pursued, who, with their prisoners and stolen livestock, were moving at a leisurely pace. As the Indian scallywags came into view, the grizzled sergeant gave an involuntary gasp of astonishment. The rascally band of Indians they had been stalking numbered at least twice the sergeant's guess, plus four white prisoners — a man, a woman and two small children. As the dauntless sergeant and his four charges rode into a clearing, the Indians saw the soldiers at the same instant that the soldiers caught sight of the Indians. The troopers quickly reined in the now blowing mounts, and executing an orderly military dismount, formed a small circle. Drawing their service revolvers, the troopers shot their faithful mounts through the head in preparation for an Indian charge they knew would not be long in coming. Although this procedure was extremely hard on cavalry mounts, it was, nevertheless, standard procedure. Horses could be replaced, but you only had one scalp and all precautions must be taken to protect it.

By the time the Indians had approached to within effective carbine range, the five gladiators in blue were well entrenched and ready to send as many Indians to their happy hunting ground as possible. No trooper gave any outward indication of the fact that the odds against their gallant little band had now leaped to seemingly overwhelming proportions.

The Indians, apparently feeling their great advantage in numbers would carry the day whenever they were ready to bring about a quick decision, took their time in charging the makeshift fort. The Indians made the fatal mistake of not charging in full force, but came on in a piecemeal fashion. In but a few ticks of the clock, the ground surrounding the embattled troopers was littered with dead and dying Sioux.

Between volleys of pistol and carbine fire, Sergeant Leonard kept searching for the four white prisoners taken by the Indians. Off in the distance he could see two Indians who had been left to guard the prisoners. Knowing Indians, Sgt. Leonard could only surmise as to how long the white prisoners would remain alive. Suddenly and without a word of warning to anyone, Sgt. Leonard leaped from behind the horse barricade and made a desperate, crouched-over dash for the cover

40

of some trees off to his left. It seemed unbelievable that anyone could reach this goal undetected, but Sgt. Leonard did.
Slowly and cautiously, he worked his way around the clearing
where the fire fight was taking place, with even now renewed
frenzy.

Still Sgt. Leonard's luck held. The two Indians left to
guard the white prisoners were so intent on watching the results of the battle taking place in the clearing, they failed to
hear or see Sgt. Leonard's stealthy approach. Resting the barrel of his big service revolver against a craggy branch of a cottonwood tree, Sgt. Leonard brought the weapon past half-cock
to full-cock, slowly, so that the click of the hammer or the
turning of the cylinder would not alert the two Indians of his
presence. Shifting a huge cud of tobacco from his left cheek to
his right cheek, Sgt. Leonard took careful aim at one of the
Indians and slowly squeezed the trigger.

The heavy caliber pistol bucked and roared as it spat out a
huge slug and sent it winging on its way. One of the two Indian guards, with a look of astonished disbelief on his face,
fumbled at his chest in a futile attempt to stem the flow of
crimson bubbling from a jagged hole that had suddenly appeared and with a death rattle in his throat, crumpled in an un-
gainly heap at his pony's feet, dead before he hit the ground,
with one of Sgt. Leonard's bullets in his heart.

The second Indian, wheeling at the sound of the shot, attempted to locate its source. Still resting his big service revolver against the tree, Sgt. Leonard shifted his weight just
enough to bring his aim to bear on the second Indian, still
frantically searching for the source of Leonard's first shot.
With his mouth extremely dry from excitement despite the tobacco, Sgt. Leonard fired again. Once more the heavy caliber
pistol belched smoke and flame. The second Indian slid from
his horse to the ground without a sound, a round black hole
directly in the center of his forehead.

Sgt. Leonard moved quickly to the four white captives
and while he was feverishly untying their bonds, he ordered
them to return to what was left of their home, wait about two

hours and if the troopers had not shown by that time, the farmer was to take his family and make all haste to the protection of the army post. Nodding their heads in frightened understanding, the prisoners rode off on the two Indian ponies. Sgt. Leonard now began his perilous *journada* back to the clearing.

By the time he had retraced his steps, the fight in the clearing had all but ended. As the Indians withdrew in ragged order, the four privates were busily engaged in taking long range pot shots at them.

A count of dead Indians lying about their defense perimeter totaled 39. Adding to this the two Indians Sgt. Leonard had dispatched added up to a tidy sum. And by some sort of a miracle, not one of the troopers had received so much as a scratch.

Rounding up some riderless Indian ponies standing about, of which there was an ample supply, the detail headed back toward the farmhouse. At the farmhouse, the farmer explained what had caused the Indians actions.

"They came looking for whiskey," he said, "and when I told them I didn't have any, they got mad and set fire to the house."

Sergeant Leonard's first official citation for the Medal of Honor reads: "Gallantry in action."

But the saga of Sergeant Patrick Leonard does not end here.

CAULDRON OF DEATH

In all of the military services of the United States, there is none which can compare, or even approach, that which was required in fighting the hostile Indians of the American West. It was a service so unlike any other that history has failed to furnish a comparison.

Privates Herman Fichter, John Kilmartin, Daniel H. Miller, John Yount and Sergeant John Mott: "Gallantry in action."

The Army calls it the Battle of the Whetstone Mountains, Arizona Territory, 5 May, 1871. We know it as the Battle of Bear Springs.

During April and May of 1871, a detail of one lieutenant, one sergeant and sixteen enlisted men from Troop F, 3rd United States Cavalry, was ordered to scout the Sononita and Santa Cruz valleys and that portion of the country bordering on the Sonora line. They first marched southeast to the Cienega Ranch, then due south to Camp Crittenden. From Camp Crittenden, the trek was continued southeast to Portrero. From Portrero they marched along the Sononita and after rounding the southwest front of the Santa Cruz Mountains, made camp at Santa Curz, New Mexico.

The commandant at Santa Cruz informed the officer-in-charge the Indians they sought could, in all probability, be located somewhere in the Huachuca Mountains. Since this was the primary purpose of their mission, the officer-in-charge of the detail was determined to go there. Leaving Santa Cruz, the small detail rode first northeast, and then north, arriving in a canyon on the east side of the Huachuca Mountains. Fresh Indian signs gave every indication their march should soon begin to bear fruit. Marching rapidly over broken and rocky country, they bivouaced in Canyon Alisos.

Because the surrounding territory had been burning for several days prior to their arrival, fresh forage for the rapidly tiring and depleted animals, was almost non.existent. It was decided to march as quickly as the animals would allow, northeast to Camp Wallen. Upon arriving at Camp Wallen, it was found this area had also been denuded and blackened by fire, which in some areas was still smouldering. With the worn animals setting the pace,and the necessity, they set out to march to Bear Springs, located deep within the Whetstone Mountains.

Almost at once they struck hot Indian signs, which appeared to be one squaw and one pony, headed in the direction of Bear Springs. Sergeant Mott and three privates were ordered to follow the tracks, while the main detachment continued on toward the spring. After following the tracks for less than a mile, they led into a deep arroyo. But something didn't seem just right to Sergeant Mott. It appeared as though the squaw, in walking through the sand, was making every effort to leave each of her footprints as clear as was possible. It appeared as though she was even avoiding stepping on rocks and stones in her efforts to do so. Sergeant Mott became convinced he was being led into a trap and decided to vacate the bottom of the canyon at once.

The four men had scarcely reached the top of the left wall of the canyon when they noticed a party of about fifteen Indians lying in wait for them in one of the main branches of the canyon. Sergeant Mott felt that from his commanding high position, three men could contain the Indians long enough for the fourth man to seek out and return with the main body of troops. As the men dismounted in preparation to positioning themselves to deliver enfilading fire on the Indians, Sgt. Mott now noticed a much larger band of Indians sneaking around to their left in an attempt to outflank them.

At this point, Sgt. Mott deemed it most prudent to execute an expedient retreat, but while the men were in the process of remounting their horses, the Indians attempting to outflank them fired a wild volley in their direction. Private Green's horse was mortally wounded and Private Pierce was severely wounded by the desultory fire. The men now hastened toward their rear, closely followed by the Indian braves. So closely were the troopers followed by the Indians, that one of them was able to ride up behind Private Green and snatch the campaign hat from his head.

The fourth trooper, who had by now signaled the main body of troops, returned to the fray and began firing his service revolver into the rear of the Indians. Thinking this fire was being delivered by the main body of troops, the Indians hesitated, allowing Sergeant Mott and the two privates enough of a respite so they could escape. This respite was short-lived, however. The Indians began to pursue the four troopers more vigorously, no doubt hoping to capture them alive, while at the same time delivering a brisk, but apparently harmless fire.

As the main body of troops arrived, they attacked the Indians at once, and a vigorous fire fight quickly ensued. However, the troopers delivered such a withering volley of fire, the Indians were compelled to retreat to the nearby hills. The officer-in-charge ordered "Forward," thinking the Indians to be completely routed. Realizing that the odds were at least fifteen to one, that the Indians were seemingly well entrenched, that the troops would be advancing over open ground, Sergeant Mott harangued the lieutenant vehemently to countermand his order. Glancing over his shoulder, the lieutenant counted himself, the sergeant and six privates.

"Eight men should be more than enough, Sergeant, order the men forward."

They advanced less than twenty yards when the Indians unleashed a hail of lead and arrows. One of the privates was struck full in the face, the ball passing out the back of his

45

head. With an ear-piercing scream, he slid from his horse to the ground, killed instantly. The lieutenant quickly ordered one of the privates to halt, and assist the fallen trooper, if he needed assistance. The assault party was now reduced to six.

Seeing such a small party advancing, the Indians rushed from their hiding places, slipping and sliding down the hill on all sides of the attacking troopers.

Sergeant Mott was about five yards in advance of the lieutenant when he heard the lieutenant say, "I am killed."

Turning, Sergeant Mott saw the lieutenant face to the rear, clasp his hands across his breast and tumble slowly to the ground. Calling to Private Fichter, they began to drag the stricken lieutenant to safety, when the officer was struck in the head and died without a sound, still in the arms of the two soldiers.

The two troopers continued to carry the dead officer's body until they caught up with Private Yount and another young private, when the latter was shot through the body, killing him instantly. The Indians, now about 50 yards away, were delivering a heavy, though sporadic fire as they continued their advance. Lowering the body of the dead lieutenant to the ground, Sergeant Mott and Private Fichter turned to face their enemy, determined to die facing their foe in the performance of their duty. Such remarkable courage caused the Indians to pause, thus enabling Privates Green and Yount to mount their horses.

Acting Corporal Kilmartin now opened a volume of fire with his small party, thus enabling Sergeant Mott and Private Fichter to mount, but scarcely had they done so, when both animals sank to the ground, riddled with rifle fire. Also killed in this volley was Private Green, his life's blood oozing from a dozen bullet wounds. Now commenced a running fight of about a mile, which drew the Indians from their cover. The brave band of men now halted to offer the Indians a front, hoping to outflank them and recover the dead bodies of their fallen comrades in arms.

As was wont with Indians, they had no stomach for battle

against determined men, preferring to skulk in ambush along the trail to Camp Crittenden.

Easily seeing through the Indians' design, which would carry the sorely pressed detachment to within a mile and a half of their position, Sergeant Mott decided it would be much the wiser if they were to circle the mountain and pick up the trail to Camp Crittenden again some four miles distant.

They crossed the Rio Babacomari about four miles above old Camp Wallen, and then continued on over the mesas, keeping the swampy headlands of the Babacomari and about a half a mile of open ground between them and the area they surmised the Indians to be lying in ambush waiting for them. When the Indians realized it was they who had been tricked, they uttered savage yells of rage and disappointment, but were utterly powerless to molest the almost spent troopers further. Although the sky was begining to darken rapidly, the troopers pushed on with all haste toward Camp Crittenden, arriving there about 1 A.M. on 6 May.

HELL'S LITTLE HALF-ACRE

The Kiowas had finally been subdued and made to settle on reservations, but not the bloodthirsty Comanches. Led by their half-breed war chief, Quanah Parker, they jumped the camp of the Fourth Cavalry on the Brazos River, near the Canyon Blanco, Texas, shortly after midnight on 9 October 1871. Before anyone was aware of the fact, the Indians were among the army horses. They had filtered through the picket guard and now the army mounts, always spooked by Indian smell, snorted and plunged in terror. Picket ropes were stretched tight and then snapped like taut wires. Picket pins hurtled through the air.

From this confused, milling mass of men and animals, the seasoned men of the Fourth regrouped and managed to beat off the attack, but not without considerable loss of horses in the process.

Lieutenant Robert G. Carter sent on a scout at dawn the next day, from a high point of land sighted some Indians busily engaged in driving off the captured army mounts in the dim gray light. With two other officers and a score of enlisted men, they galloped off in pursuit of the fleeing savages. A chase of several miles led them into a deep ravine of the Canyon Blanco. No sooner had the steep walls of the canyon closed in to engulf the little band, than Indians sprang up on all sides of them. The men, realizing their mounts were too jaded to affect a successful withdrawal under fire, dismounted

49

and deployed in a well-disciplined manner and opened fire at close range.

The Indians, gaudily daubed with war paint, assuming they had the soldiers trapped, circled the men slowly, howling and shooting, while the squaws screeched and wailed encouragement from the heights above.

Lieutenant Carter, barely managing to hold one flank of the line with a sergeant and four privates, had just finished putting fresh cartridges in the cylinder of his service pistol when he looked up in horrified disbelief to see the rest of the officers and men suddenly mount up and gallop off. The screaming Comanches quickly began to close in upon Carter and his men. There was no other recourse for them but to mount up and attempt a running fight.

The men, all seasoned veterans, coolly obeyed Lieut. Carter's command to mount up and loading and firing their weapons with a calm determination, rode back out of the canyon, keeping up a steady, deadly fire all the while. One of the privates took a bullet in the hand, which shattered it to a pulp, but he still managed to make a good account of himself with one arm. Steadily, and with nerves of steel and skill, Lieut. Carter, keeping his command together and under control, slowly extricated himself from the canyon by falling inexorably back toward the arroyo's mouth.

As the men neared freedom, they commenced an intense volume of fire and prodded their blowing mounts into greater speed. Before this sudden and unexpected furious onslaught, the Comanches reeled back, creating a gap to freedom. Jaded mounts were prodded for still more speed. Another one of the privates shuddered from the impact of an Indian bullet, but managed to stay seated in the saddle and continue on. They were almost in the free when they were called upon to pay their toll.

Trooper Gregg shouted that his horse was all but played out. Thundering up behing the stumbling horse of Trooper Gregg came Quanah Parker, brandishing a pistol, face livid with rage. Lieut. Carter and the others reined in, vainly trying to cover the doomed man whose body masked their fire. Trooper Gregg was frantically tugging at his holstered service revolver when Quanah Parker placed his pistol at the base of Trooper Gregg's skull and squeezed the trigger. The gun flamed and the soldier toppled from his saddle, dead before he hit the ground. Lieut. Carter and the remainder of his pitiful command rode clear.

The rest of the regiment rode into the fray and almost had the Comanches cornered when a heavy snowstorm descended and allowed the Indians to slink away.

Carter, Robert G., Second Lieutenant, Fourth United States Cavalry. On Brazos River, Texas, 10 October 1871, "Held the left of the line with a few men during the charge of a large body of Indians, after the right of the line had retreated, and by delivering a rapid fire succeeded in checking the enemy until other troops came to the rescue."

WHAT IS VALOR?

The strength of America's Army has always been in the spirit of the individual soldier. The acts of extraordinary courage, to which we pay tribute, were not performed in the hope of reward. They began with a soldier doing his duty.

In the spring of 1872, two great railroads were being pushed across the seemingly endless flatlands of the Great Southwest. Stretched out over hundreds of miles of emptiness, were small groups of surveyors, engineers, contractors and other small parties necessary for the laying of track. All were subject to raids by roving bands of Comanches.

Before they were finally subdued, the Comanches had killed more whites proportionally than any other tribe of Indians on the North American continent. The Comanches were not wont to fight like the mighty Sioux to the north, or like their blood-thirsty neighbors to the east, the Cheyennes, or the Apache to the west. The Comanches seldom, if ever, participated in a headlong charge. Seldom did they allow themselves to become engaged in pitched battles, but preferred to use hit-and-run tactics, like the harassing of the flanks and rear of the small supply trains sent out to provision the railroad building parties. Terribly small in numbers compared to some of the other haughty Indian tribes, and quite poor, even by Indian standards, the Comanches were, nevertheless, extremely good fighters, composed the hardest of enemies and worthiest of foes.

William Wilson was born in Philadelphia, Pennsylvania. One of many children, and from a rather poor family, he joined the Army at an early age. By 1872, through honest, faithful and devoted service, as a soldier of good character, he had attained the rank of sergeant. He had brown hair, brown eyes, was dark complected and was five feet seven and one-half inches tall.

Springs were usually cool, crisp and clear, in the Panhandle section of Texas, and the spring of 1872 was no exception. As the sun converted itself into a magenta-colored sphere of fire, thrusting itself over the peaks of the nearby mountains on the 26th day of March, Sergeant Wilson led a detachment of twenty soldiers from Troop I, Fourth United States Cavalry Regiment, out the gates of Fort Concho, Texas. Cattle thieves had been quite active in the area. It had been reported that a bunch of renegade Mexicans had joined forces with a band of troublesome Indians. This posed a serious problem for the military.

Sgt. Wilson's mission was to find this particular group identified as being responsible for the recent and numerous depredations and return them to the fort, in chains if necessary, to answer charges.

After two fruitless days of patroling the Colorado Valley area of the Texas Panhandle, Sgt. Wilson noticed a small, but turbulent cloud of dust, on the horizon. Unlike the big battles in the woods and hills to the north, here in the panhandle there was little more than just flat plain with no appreciable rise of ground or grove of trees in which to hide behind. Any form of strategy was, therefore, almost nonexistent. The only tactic which had met with any degree of success in the past was to chase your foe until you caught him and then fight it out. Sgt. Wilson and his detail of troopers proceeded to do just that.

Advancing across the open ground at the full gallop, the troopers could see the cloud of dust was being stirred up by a few dozen head of cattle that were being driven by a small band of Mexicans and Comanches.

When the scallywags saw they were being pursued, everything was forgotten but the thought of getting away. Abandoning their ill-gotten plunder in frantic haste to escape, the renegades whipped their mounts into a frenzied dead run and headed straight for the sanctuary of the Colorado River. Behind it was Comanche territory and safety.

Sgt. Wilson shouted for one-half of his men to stay behind to round up the now scattered cattle and then continue to protect them, while he and the remainder of the detail continued to give chase to the now rapidly fleeing scamps. If he could bring back one of these rascals alive, the prisoner might be induced to talk and reveal the location of the outlaw camp. If they could locate the enemy camp, the recovery of many stolen cattle and other goods might prove possible. With these thoughts in mind, Sgt. Wilson continued his hot pursuit.

As the pursuers closed to within effective firing range of the pursued, a rifle and pistol duel on horseback ensued. Suddenly one of Sgt. Wilson's bullets found its mark.

A Comanche threw up his arms, emitted a blood-curdling scream, and pitched headlong from his horse, as a small round black hole appeared under his left shoulder blade.

Sgt. Wilson made no attempt to rein in his mount. He knew there was no need to stop for this Indian. Even if his bullet had not been fatal, it was quite obvious to the veteran sergeant from the way the Indian had been hurtled from his horse, his neck had been broken by the fall and he would do no talking, this or any other day.

In their desperate attempt to escape being overtaken by the hard riding troopers, the fleeing band of renegades tried an old ruse. They split up into three separate groups in a desperate attempt to shake Sgt. Wilson's dogged pursuit. Still thundering across the prairie at a dangerous breakneck full gallop, Sgt. Wilson frantically gestured for his men to follow suit, while he himself sped after one group, consisting of three Mexicans.

Once more Sgt. Wilson fired his service revolver. One of the renegades' horses was hit. It stumbled, then fell heavily, tossing its rider to the ground. The fallen Mexican appeared

55

shaken, but unhurt. Sgt. Wilson brought his blowing mount to a rearing halt, quickly dismounted and tied the stunned Mexican's hands and feet. As the determined Wilson was straightening up after finishing his knot-tying job, he noticed two fugitives had stopped and were sitting on their ponies perfectly still, about six-hundred yards away. Not another soul was in sight. The rest of Sgt. Wilson's troopers had raced off in different directions in pursuit of other marauders.

Without a moment's hesitation, Sgt. Wilson removed his carbine from its saddle scabbard and put a bullet into the brain of the Mexican's pain-racked horse. The animal's foreleg had been broken in the fall. Even before the poor beast's convulsive heaving had ceased, Sgt. Wilson had dropped down behind the animal to wait.

The other two thieves that Wilson had been chasing rode away from each other with the apparent intention of attempting to outflank Wilson's precarious position from both sides.

Although they were not yet within killing range, the crusty Sergeant spat a stream of black tobacco juice against a flat rock, where it sizzled in the hot sun, took careful aim at the rider on his right and waited. Exercising a trained patience born of discipline, Sgt. Wilson waited until his target was well within telling range, as the two Mexicans charged him in his horse-fort. Sgt. Wilson slowly and steadily squeezed the trigger of his carbine. Almost before the heavy caliber slug had cleared the end of the carbine barrel on its way to thud into the chest of the first Mexican, Sgt. Wilson wheeled to his left and drew down on the second charging Mexican. When the second Mexican saw the deadly accuracy of Wilson's fire, he quickly reined in his mount, and thinking discretion as the better course to follow, beat a hasty retreat toward the river.

Sgt. Wilson picked up his reluctant prisoner, hoisted him aboard the horse, mounted up behind and headed back toward Fort Concho. The rest of Wilson's detail straggled back to the fort with the cattle, but no more prisoners. The Mexican Sgt. Wilson had captured did talk and reveal the location of the thieves' camp. Sgt. Wilson's heroic exploits allowed the recovery of many stolen cattle and the roving band of renegades was broken up permanently.

In the cold and simple vernacular of the military at the time, Sgt. Wilson's official citation for the Medal of Honor reads: "Gallantry in pursuit of a band of cattle thieves from New Mexico."

But Sgt. Wilson was not yet done earning his eighteen dollars a month and beans. The summer had passed without any major incidents as far as Sgt. Wilson and the 4th were concerned. But now it was September and the nights had become chilly, as they always do in the Texas Panhandle.

The Comanche raids on the railroad parties had been stepped up.

The 4th was ordered out in force, to find the raiders and end their depredations once and for all. The 4th marched the entire length of the Llano Estacada (Staked Plains), all the way to Fort Bascom, New Mexico. Nothing! After a rest and a change of horses, the 4th was back in the saddle once more. Little more than a day's ride out of Fort Bascom on their return trip to Fort Concho, as the regiment prepared to cross the North Fork of the Red River, near McClellan's Creek on September 29th, advance patrols reported sighting a large Comanche camp a few miles downstream. Fearing any delay might give the Indians a chance to prepare a defense, an attack by the entire 4th, in force, was immediately ordered.

The plan of attack was quite simple. Since the Comanche camp was located directly on the river's bank, a charge would be undertaken directly along the river. Troop I was selected to lead the charge. Once in position, Troop I would stop and hold the ground immediately in front of the Indian camp. The rest of the regiment was to swing around and encircle the Indian camp on the two sides. The Indians would thus be surrounded on three sides, with their backs to the river. The well-disciplined, precision-perfect attack launched by Troop I was a textbook jewel and a thing to behold. It caught the Comanches completely by surprise. Best of all, the day might have been won without firing a shot, were it not for those unexpected non-tangibles that seem to pop up occasionally when least expected.

The impossible probable that was to haunt Troop I was to earn Sgt. Wilson his second Medal of Honor.

Troop I had just about captured its desired position in front of the Indian camp, when one of the officers' horses seemed to fall away from him. As the officer fought desperately to stay in the saddle, out of the corner of his eye, he noticed several other troopers encountering the same difficulty. Like flies caught on flypaper, Troop I had unwittingly blundered into that dreadful nightmare—QUICKSAND!

Within the wink of an eye, Sgt. Wilson suddenly found himself the only officer or non-commissioned officer available to command. Troop I held the key position to the whole attack in keeping the Indians surrounded and held at bay. Sgt. Wilson knew Troop I was supposed to hold its ground once it was in position. Sgt. Wilson held.

The Comanches, given an unexpected reprieve, however, struck at Troop I with savage fury. The Comanches quickly realized their only hope of escaping the encircling blue-clad troopers rested on their dislodging Troop I, without undue delay, from its not too tenable position along the river bank.

For three long, agonizing hours, while the rest of the regiment completed its encircling maneuver, and then fought its way into the Indian camp proper, Sgt. Wilson and Troop I held its ground against desperate attack.

Carbines became so hot the troopers were almost unable to hold them. Water from drinking canteens was poured over their barrels to cool them off. Service pistols boomed almost incessantly, as the Comanches tried trick after trick to no avail, against the tenacious Wilson and his determined men.

First the Indians tried to rush the hastily barricaded troops in force, hoping to overrun the puny detail blocking their path to freedom. Sgt. Wilson and his men cut gaping holes in the Indians' lines, and Troop I held. Failing in their attempt at a frontal attack, the Indians now tried stealthy infiltration.

Thwarting every scheme the Indians attempted, Troop I held its ground.

Once again the Comanches came in force, emitting hideous war cries, as only an Indian, especially a Comanche, could utter. They asked no quarter and received none.

Sgt. Wilson ordered his men to use the bodies of dead Indians as breastworks. Troop I held.

One brave, but foolish Indian crept to within a few feet of the spot Sgt. Wilson had chosen as his temporary command headquarters. Waiting an opportunity when the sergeant's attention was directed elsewhere conducting command of the defense, the Indian lunged at Wilson with a bloodchilling cry on his lips and a vicious looking knife in his hand.

Some inner instinct born of experience caused the veteran sergeant to turn to face the Indian in time. Rolling over and over on the ground, while bullets whistled and sung overhead, the two men struggled desperately for possession of the knife.

After what seemed like an eternity of struggling, the boneweary and almost completely exhausted sergeant, by some superhuman effort, managed to turn the Indian's own knife against him. Then without so much as a word or backward glance at his fallen foe, Sgt. Wilson struggled back to his position of command and continued to give orders as though nothing had happened.

The Indians, unable to dislodge Troop I, completely surrounded by determined men on three sides, finally attacked the river to escape. In their near panic rout to escape the vengeful troopers, the Indians left women and children huddled and cringing in their teepees.

The regiment made no attempt to follow. The fighting had been of the heaviest variety and the 4th was pretty well spent, so they decided to hold the ground they had battled so valiantly to attain. Besides, without supplies or water, no one, not even an Indian, could long survive on the plains of Texas.

A few days later, the Indians began to straggle back to surrender. It was the first time in seventeen years of warfare, along the length of the Texas plains, that Comanches had officially asked for peace.

The railroads went through and Sgt. Wilson was awarded his second Medal of Honor, with the official citation reading: "Distinguished conduct in action with Indians."

NONE BUT THE VALIANT

To write about individuals who perform acts of heroism in human conflict, without becoming overly superfluous or repetitious, is quite difficult.

It was during the winter campaigns of 1872-73, at the battle of Salt River Cave, that First Sergeant James Blair, Sergeant James E. Bailey, Sergeant Clay Beauford, Sergeant William L. Day, Sergeant William Osborne, Sergeant Lehman Hinemann, Sergeant Henry J. Hyde, Sergeant Rudolph von Medem, Private James W. Huff, Private Moses Orr and Indian Scouts Nantaje, Achesay, Blanquet, Elsatsoosu, Kelsay, Kosoha, Machol, Nannasaddie, Chiquito and Jim were awarded Medals of Honor for: "Gallant conduct during campaigns and engagements with Apaches."

By the winter of 1872, the campaign against the Apaches was going on in earnest. Those blood-lusting warriors had departed the valley of the Salt and Gila Rivers in southern Arizona and then vanished into the rugged country of the Tonto Basin, where they knew every rock and cactus.

On a bleak and dreary Christmas Day, Major Brown, with troops B and E of the 5th Cavalry and also 30 Apache scouts, rendezvoused with Captain Burns, who commanded 40 troopers and nearly 100 Indian scouts from the Pima Tribe, somewhere in the vicinity of present-day Roosevelt Dam. During the evening of 27 December, as the men rested and cared for animals and equipment, the men were made aware of the main object of their expedition.

It had long been a known fact, the Indians had a well-concealed hiding place somewhere in the rugged country in or near the Salt River Canyon. One of the Apache scouts named Nantaje told of living in a huge cave when he was a youth growing up, in the general area in which the military would be searching. He agreed to lead the troops there but only on his own terms. It was decided that only the ablest of men would make up the detail destined to make an attack. They would carry only the barest of necessities along with their arms and extra ammunition. The trek through the Mazatzal Range and subsequent descent into the Salt River Gorge, was to be made at night, on foot, with each man donning moccasins to insure a minimum of noise, was certain to exert even the most well conditioned of troopers.

With mixed and brooding misgivings about being led on such a mission with an uncertain Apache guide, the band of picked men set out along the treacherous trail, knowing only too well how vulnerable their position would be should their presence become known to the Indian they sought, or, if they were being led into a trap. The men's pent-up anxiety almost reached its zenith when fresh footprints were discovered which, much to their relief, upon close examination proved to be bear tracks.

As they neared their objective, Nantaje advised the officer-in-charge to send some of his best marksmen on ahead because a small party would have a much better chance of approaching their objective undetected. Fifteen volunteers, accompanied by Nantaje himself, crept stealthily around the face of a cliff where they came upon such a weird scene as to almost be unbelievable.

High up one of the precipitous canyon walls, perhaps about 200 feet below the crest of the canyon rim, was the dark indentation of a wide, but shallow cave. In the opening before the cave, a party of Indian raiders cavorted before a small fire, their shadows dancing monstrous and grotesque contortions against the overhanging cliffs. One look at the cave and its location made it easy to see why the Indians had so often been able to elude pursuit from the military and then from the security of their retreat, laugh silently as they watched the frustrated soldiers struggling through the canyon below.

The men were able to creep within a few yards of the cave, so confident were the Indians of their not being discovered and so intent were they on their victory celebration.

Came a whispered command, "Ready! Aim! Fire!!!"

Six of the Indians prancing before the fire danced to the tune of death in that first excited volley. The rest rushed panic-stricken to the rear of the cave.

Not too far away the main column heard the crash of the pistol fire. In the narrow confines of the canyon walls and the deathlike stillness of the night, it sounded like a thunderous barrage of mountain howitzers. Aware now that contact had been made, but not knowing the situation, forty men were hurried forward from the main command to act as reinforcements, should they become necessary. The troopers were extremely fortunate that no one fell to his death in their wild scrambles around the near vertical sides of the canyon. However, despite all the hazards, they valiantly managed to effect a junction with the original party of volunteers, who were now busily engaged as a deterrent in bottling up the now sufficiently recovered Indians, who, even at this moment, were planning a counterattack.

As the rest of the main force hurried forward, they quickly took up holding positions. One half of the troopers were posted in a flanking position, taking their stand behind some rock about 30 to 40 yards back from the entrance to the cave.

When all of the troopers were well entrenched, the Indians were called upon to surrender. Their answer was to hurl shouts of derision, taunts, threats and insults at the troopers. They shouted they would rather die than surrender.

The troopers prepared to help them out.

Each side took stock of its own situation. The Indians were well supplied and located in an excellent defensive position. A natural rock wall about ten feet high dropped off from the outer edge of the floor of the cave into a steep sloping gully. On the other hand, the troopers held a local advantage in numbers plus control of the situation at present, which, at best, was only temporary. They had no supplies and the possibilities of the Indians being reinforced mounted with each passing moment. As they were in control of the situation, if they intended to remain so, immediate and drastic action was called for on the part of the troopers.

Suddenly one of the men had an idea. Soon all the troopers began to fire their pistols as fast as they could reload them at the slanting roof of the cave. It didn't take long before ricocheting bullets and flying rock fragments began to exact a toll among the Indians. The troopers ceased firing and once again the Indians were called upon to surrender.

The weird chant that began to issue from the cave was one the seasoned frontier fighters had never heard before. It sounded like half wail, half exultation. There was a warning cry from the Apache scouts.

"Look out, it is the death chant. They will charge."

Over the rampart charged twenty savage warriors, each armed with a bow and arrows and rifle. Half of the near-naked warriors stood bodly atop the bulwark, blazing away in an attempt to draw the fire of the troopers away from the others, who were attempting to break through on the troopers' right flank.

The soldiers in the front ranks rushed forward to close with the Indians, with a hatred that possibly surpassed that of the Indians.

Six of the Indians fell dead and the others fell back to the safety of the cave.

Yet in the ensuing confusion, the Indian succeeded in slipping through the blue line, and then made a fatal mistake. The Indian could not resist hurling a taunt at the soldiers. He stopped and turned to hurl his taunt, when too late he saw the second line of troopers. He was literally cut to ribbons by a volley of carbine fire.

The troopers now massed for a charge designed to dislodge the Indians once and for all.

While the heavy fighting had been taking place in front of the cave, another part of the main command had been patrolling other canyons in the vicinity, searching for more hostiles. Hearing the gunfire, they too hastened toward the main canyon. As they picked their way over the torturous terrain, Dame Fortune led them to approach on top of the cliff above the cave. Leaning over the cliff, they took the situation in at a glance.

The Apaches were lying close to the outer edge of the ledge, fronting the cave opening in an effort to avoid the deadly missiles of glancing lead and flying rock. This left them exposed to the fire of those overhead.

A safety line, constructed of the men's suspenders, was quickly put together so that two of the troopers could lean out over the precipice to fire revolvers at the enemy below. This tactic was bringing results until the men got excited and began throwing the revolvers at the Indians. Someone then suggested that boulders would be less expensive than revolvers, so the men began to throw boulders over the edge of the cliff. Harassed by the fire from below, and the boulders from above, the defenders of the cave began to fall, one by one.

Through the clouds of dust and dense black powder smoke, an old medicine man could be seen calmly crouched behind a rock, answering the fire of the troopers with a steady volley of his own. Then he too, like all of the rest, disappeared from sight and all signs of resistance ceased. An ominous silence fell over the entire scene.

A charge was ordered and, as the troopers leaped the parapet, they fully expected to be met by a hail of lead and arrows from some hidden recess in the cave, but the only audible sounds came from those of the wounded. It seemed impossible that anyone could have survived that holocaust of fire, but thirty-five Indians were found still alive.

Today, the gorge of the Salt River is partly filled with the waters of Canyon Lake.

DESPERATE JOURNEY

Major John Green, First United States Cavalry, "In order to reassure his command, this officer, in the most fearless manner and, exposed to very great danger, walked in front of the line; the command, thus encouraged, advanced over the lava upon the Indians who were concealed among the rocks."

Contract Surgeon John O. Skinner, United States Army, "Rescued a wounded soldier who lay under a close and heavy fire during the assault on the Modoc stronghold after two soldiers had unsuccessfully attempted to make the rescue and both had been wounded in dong so."

After the treachery of Captain Jack and the Modoc Indians at the Lava Beds in California, the Army was almost crazy for revenge.

The Indians could not be allowed to get away with downright, out-and-out murder. If the Indians who perpetrated such a dastardly deed were not apprehended, and at once, every redskin west of the Mississippi River would don fresh war paint. With its usual unglamorous, bulldog tenacity, the army soon forced the Indians, to vacate their powerful, natural stronghold, the Lava Beds. Then, for six long days, the scouting parties could find nothing.

Come 17 January 1873, the scouting party topped a small hill, which looked like it would make a good artillery position in case of trouble, and then broke for lunch. Suddenly and unlooked for, a volley of fire lashed into the unsuspecting troopers. The soldiers appeared to be doomed.

Modocs had sneaked in on all sides of them, had them completely surrounded in an extremely poor defensive position and their bullets were cutting troopers down one by one. In a short period of time, only twenty men remained fit for duty, out of the original eighty-five.

Captain Evan Thomas kept steadying the ever-dwindling knot of survivors.

"Steady, men, we are surrounded, but let us keep our face to the enemy and die like brave men."

Captain Thomas fell dead along with all of the other officers, but the men continued to fight.

Major John Green with the main command heard the firing and was rushing to the aid of the besieged men with all possible speed. They reached the battle ground late in the afternoon, in time to save what was left of the scouting party. All that night, the troopers held the position. In the morning's light it was discovered the Indians had left. The troops retired from the field carrying their dead and wounded.

CHECKMATE

General Crook had deployed his forces in such a manner that no matter what the Apaches might try to do, he could be after them, in force, at once. So when the red devils caught a party of white civilians unawares, killed all but two, tied these to cactus plants and shot them full of arrows, the army was on the move.

The twenty-Third Infantry Regiment found itself in closest pursuit of the Indians. After a long, hard march, the men of the 23rd ran the Apaches to ground near Turret Butte, Arizona, on 27 March 1873.

Now Turret Butte was a natural fort. A plateau with precipitous slopes which appeared to be almost unclimbable. To attempt any kind of a daylight storming of the Indians' position could only result in disaster to the soldiers. They decided to use one of the Indians' tricks and attack by night.

Preserving an unbelievable, exceptionally extraordinary quiet, hour upon hour, the troopers hauled themselves and their equipment up the steep heights. By midnight they were all in position on the summit. They settled down in the mountain cold to wait the dawn, shivering and silent. At dawn the bugle blew the signal to charge. It was as stunning a victory as the army had ever achieved. Volley after volley was poured into the milling Apaches.

Unable to move, with every retreat skillfully blocked by troopers, the Apaches surrendered.

THEY STOOD THEIR GROUND

First Sergeant William Allen, 23rd Infantry; First Sergeant James M. Hill, 5th Cavalry; Private Eben Stanley, 5th Cavalry; Sergeant Daniel Bishop, 23rd Infantry: "Gallantry in action."

DeArmond, William, Sergeant, Company I, 5th U.S. Infantry, Upper Washita River, Texas, 9 September 1874, "Gallantry in action."

Hay, Fred S., Sergeant, Company I, 5th U.S. Infantry, Upper Washita River, Texas, 9-11 September 1874, "Gallantry in action."

James, John, Corporal, Company I, 5th U.S. Infantry, Upper Washita River, Txas, 9-11 September 1874, "Gallantry in action."

Kelly, John J. H., Private, Company I, 5th U.S. Infantry, Upper Washita River, Texas, 9 September 1874, "Gallantry in action."

Kelly, Thomas, Private, Company I, 5th U.S. Infantry, Upper Washita River, Texas, 9 September 1874, "Gallantry in action."

Kitchen, George K., Sergeant, Troop K, 6th U.S. Cavalry, Upper Washita River, Texas, 9 September 1874, "Gallantry in action."

Knox, John W., Corporal, Company I, 5th U.S. Infantry, Upper Washita River, Texas, 9 September 1874, "Gallantry in action."

Koelpin, William, Sergeant, Company I, 5th U.S. Infantry, Upper Washita River, Texas, 9-11 September 1874, "Gallantry in action."

Morris, William W., Corporal, Troop H, 6th U.S. Cavalry, Upper Washita River, Texas, 9-11 September 1874, "Gallantry in action."

Pennsyl, Joshiah, Sergeant, Troop M, 6th U.S. Cavalry, Upper Washita River, Texas, 11 September 1874, "Gallantry in action."

Sharpless, Edward C., Corporal, Troop H, 6th U.S. Cavalry, Upper Washita River, Texas, 9-11 September 1874, "Gallantry in action."

Singleton (Neilon), Frank, Sergeant, Troop A, 6th U.S. Cavalry, at Washita River, Texas, 9-11 September 1874, "Gallantry in action."

Woodall, Zachariah, Sergeant, Troop I, 6th U.S. Cavalry, at Washita River, Texas, 12 September 1874: "While in command of five men and carrying dispatches, was attacked by 125 Indians whom he, with his command, fought throughout the day, he being severely wounded."

Harrington, John, Private, Troop H, 6th U.S. Cavalry, at Washita River, Texas, 12 September 1874: "While carrying dispatches was attacked by 125 hostile Indians, whom he, and his comrades, fought throughout the day."

Roth, Peter, Private, Troop A, 6th U.S. Cavalry, at Washita River, Texas, 12 September 1874, "Gallantry in action."

Smith, George W., Private, Troop M. 6th U.S. Cavalry, at Washita River, Texas, 12 September 1874, "Gallantry in action."

In the spring of 1874, Kiowa, Comanche and Cheyenne Indians banded together to vent their wrath on a score-and-a half of white buffalo hunters at a remote spot called Adobe Walls, an abandoned trading post on the Canadian River in the Texas Panhandle. The attack turned out to be a humiliating defeat for the Indians, who then scattered out across the Texas Plains, bent on quenching their thirst for plunder and revenge.

As Indian depredations began to increase alarmingly in both size and number, the military began mapping plans for a vigorous campaign to force the marauders back to the reservations. What later was to become known as the Red River War, called for a five-pronged sweep deep into the Indian lair, which lay well into the heart of the Texas Panhandle, between the Canadian and the Washita Rivers. It resulted in a most unbelievable and bizarre sequence of events that can be imagined.

By late August 1874, heavy rains had given new life to the parched prairie grass. With the lands once more lush and green, a commodity essential to provide forage for the animals, on 26 August a long-awaited drive was launched against the hostiles. One column moved west from Fort Sill, Oklahoma Territory. Another column moved north from Fort Clark. Still another column moved from Fort Griffin. Major Price marched down the Canadian River and Colonel Nelson A. Miles left Camp Supply with eight troops of the 6th Cavalry and four companies of the 5th Infantry.

A prominent Indian trail was discovered almost at once by the scouts of Colonel Miles' command. It pointed southwest. The men hastened in pursuit.

On the morning of August 30th, a five-hour clash was fought about twelve miles from the Red River. The Indians fled up one of the many craggy branches of the Palo Duro Canyon, separated into small bands and erupted out onto the Staked Plains.

Military supplies began to run dangerously low. The animals needed a rest as they were in no condition for a prolonged campaign on the arid tablelands of the Staked Plains which lay ahead.

Colonel Miles was determined to continue the chase for a while at least. He just could not stomach the thought of breaking off the chase once the trail had become hot. He dispatched his wagons back to Camp Supply for a restocking. The wagons wheeled about on September 1st.

Meanwhile, the Indians had wandered about aimlessly for

several days trying to decide what they wanted to do. On the morning of September 8th, an Indian youth was sent back along the trail to search for wayward ponies. The youth was taken prisoner by some army scouts carrying dispatches for Colonel Miles.

One of these scouts was a Lieutenant named Frank D. Baldwin, who just one month away, would receive his second Medal of Honor. The scouts returned with their reluctant prisoner to the main supply column about mid-morning of September 9th.

The Indians waited all day of September 8th for the youth to return. When he failed to do so, they sent out search parties. Lieut. Baldwin's trail was easy to follow, and it led them straight to the main supply column. The Indians were first sighted by the main body about 8 A.M. on the morning of September 9th, when they opened fire on the supply wagons at long range. A series of spirited charges by small raiding parties of trooper soon drove the Indians off. By 2 P.M., the supply wagons were about two miles from the Washita River. As the supply wagons slowly emerged from a ravine, the Indians prepared to attack.

Captain Wyllys Lyman had 36 wagons moving in a double column, about twenty yards apart. On either flank marched a file from Company I, 5th U.S. Infantry. Leading the column were thirteen men of the 6th U.S. Cavalry. The wagons were immediately ordered to corral. Conforming to the existing terrain, the wagons formed a crescent-shaped enclosure. The infantry guarded the flanks while the cavalry protected the rear. The soldiers hastily dug rifle pits around the perimeter and otherwise fortified themselves as best they could. It was none too soon. The Indians charged with savage fury.

Sergeant William DeArmond collapsed to the ground, his left knee shattered by an Indian bullet, yet he refused to leave his position in the firing line where he continued to direct the defense. Lieutenant Lewis fell dead. Here and there a trooper clutched at a wound and fell from the line. Veteran Sergeant

Frederick S. Hay took over command of Lieutenant Lewis' men.

For a moment it appeared as though the Indians might break through the ring of gallant and intrepid men, but they stood their ground, refusing to yield a thing. From such determination, the Indians withdrew.

While harassing fire kept the soldiers' heads down, mounted braves began to circle the beleaguered wagons.

Keeping his wits about him and not letting the Indians panic him into a rash move, Captain Lyman directed a defense of his wagons, while repulsing savage attacks from all quarters. On the right, accurate fire directed by First Sergeant John Mitchell drove the warriors back with heavy losses. As darkness approached, the soldiers settled themselves in for a siege. Departing from their usual tactics of disappearing after their initial attack had been repulsed, the Indians also dug in for a siege.

All day, September 10th, the Indians resorted to sporadic harassing fire, evidently intent only on keepng the supply wagons from their intended destination. Sergeant Frank (Neilon) Singleton took a bullet in the leg. September 11th came and went. September 12th. Still the men stood their ground.

On September 13th, the Indians began to tire of slow siege tactics and started to drift away to the southwest.

By 2:30 A.M., on September 14th, the supply column was once more on the move to keep its long delayed rendezvous with Colonel Miles. Unbeknown to the defenders of the supply wagons, sometime during the darkened hours of September 13th, a scouting party from Major Price's column out of Fort Union, New Mexico, passed close to the besieged wagons, but proceeded without notice.

Colonel Miles had camped on the banks of McClellan's Creek on September 8th, to await the return of his supply wagons. On September 10th, when the supply wagons still had not shown, Colonel Miles ordered two of his best civilian scouts to ride to Camp Supply and report his supplies still hadn't arrived. William (Billy) Dixon and Amos Chapman were accompanied by four troopers. (It was the same Billy Dixon who had been one of the heroes of the Adobe Walls fight.) The small party left the camp on McClellan's Creek at sundown on September 10th. They rode by night and hid by day. At sunrise of the second day (September 12th), as they topped a small rise, they came face-to-face with approximately 125 Kiowa and Comanche warriors—another one of the small bands which had only recently left the siege of Lyman's wagons.

With no place to hide, the small group was quickly surrounded, their mounts being much too jaded to make a run for it. Death seemed almost a certainty, but the indomitable spirit of America's fighting men made them determined to at least die fighting.

Private Smith was put in charge of the horses, and he went down in the first Indian volley, horribly wounded in the chest. As he slumped to the ground, uncontrollable hands released the horses reins and his rifle dropped to the ground out of reach. Within a span of less than 30 minutes, every member of the party had received wounds to some extent. Besides Smith, Chapman fell with a shattered left knee. Dixon took an arrow in the calf of his leg, yet only Smith and Chapman were disabled.

To stay on that little hill was sure death, but where were they to hide? Cover was next to non-existent. Glancing about, Dixon noted a buffalo wallow about ten feet in diameter, but a few short feet away. It was slight in depth, but it would be better than where they were. Those that could jumped up and made a dash for the wallow with bullets whipping about them like angry hornets. As each man leaped into the depression, he began digging furiously with hands or knife to deepen the hole. As it had been at Adobe Walls, Dixon's deadly and accurate fire kept the Indians from collecting any of the heroic band's scalps, as the wallow was slowly made deeper. Although enclosed on all sides by an overwhelming number of hostile Indians, they succeeded, while under an intense fire at short range, in digging with knives and hands, this slight cover.

Smith and Chapman still lay on the prairie unable to move. As the wallow became deep enough to afford some semblance of cover, Dixon leaped from the hole and carried Chapman in, dodging a hail of bullets in the process. Smith lay quite a bit further from the wallow, where he had taken the bullet in the chest. His rifle, which had dropped from his hand, became a much sought-after prize by the Indians. One after another, as each Indian crept forward and tried to claim the gun, was cut down by Dixon's unerring aim. By noon of September 12, their ammunition began to run dangerously low. Roth volunteered to fetch Smith's cartridge belt, which was still full. The Indians still continued to circle them without let-up. Roth dashed to Smith's body and returned to the wallow-fort with the astonishing news, that Smith was still alive. Dixon and Roth dashed to Smith and returned to the hole with bullets kicking up dust all around them.

Smith was sat in an upright position to conceal the crippled condition of the party. From early morning until dark, under an almost constant fire from the Indians and at such short range the beleaguered men often were able to use their pistols, this gallant detail defended their lives and that of their dying comrades, their only drink being the scant amount of stinking, dirty and tepid water that collected in the bottom of the hollow they had made. The men, exhausted and thirsty, drooping under the burning sun, continued to reach into their dwindling supply of cartridges.

The simple recital of their deeds and the mention of odds against which they fought, how the wounded defended the dying, and how the dying aided the wounded by exposure to new wounds after the power of movement had been taken away. These alone present a scene of cool courage, heroism and self-sacrifice, which duty prompts us to recognize but which we cannot fully honor. A medal is not much weighed against a man's life, but it is all that we have to offer.

By noon the thirst of the small group had become almost

unbearable. The assault waves had dashed forward and ebbed against the buffalo-wallow bulwarks. Then clouds formed, thunder and lightning stabbed the sky, and a typical Panhandle torrential rain began to fall. A brisk breeze sprang up from the north, chilling the bedraggled band to the bone. The sudden change in weather proved to be the salvation of the seemingly doomed men.

Most Indians hated rain and cold weather. These were no different and they withdrew without ceremony.

The men had lost all of their personal equipment when the horses had stampeded from Smith's drying grip. The small group faced a bleak and somber situation: tired, hungry, cold, thirsty, wounded, ammunition low and no relief in sight—but they continued to stand their ground. As darkness approached. Dixon and Roth gathered up some tumbleweeds and stamped them into the bottom of the hole, as a shield against the damp cold. The group could only sit and suffer through the hours of darkness, not knowing the Indians had disappeared, flushed also by Major Price's column.

Soon after dark, Private Smith fell asleep and about 1:00 A.M., he died. His body was lifted tenderly out of the hole, and his face covered with a bandana.

The next morning, September 13th, with no Indians in sight, Dixon left the hole in search of help, and he stumbled upon Major Price's column.

A relief party returned to the wallow and was fired upon by the men, thinking the Indians had returned.

Private Smith was wrapped in an army blanket and buried in the buffalo wallow he helped to hallow. He lies there today.

The other five men all wounded, were returned to Camp Supply, where Chapman's leg had to be amputated above the knee. Dixon remained with the army as a scout until 1883, when he homesteaded a claim which included the ruins of Adobe Walls. All the others remained in the army except Chapman.

All six men were requested to be awarded the Medal of Honor for their participation in the Buffalo Wallow Fight, for what Colonel Miles called "an instance of indomitable courage, skill and true heroism."

However, Dixon and Chapman did not receive Medals as they were scouts in the employ of the Army and did not belong to the Army. The requirements for earning the Medal clearly states, "men in uniform." One government official of the times stated it was a flagrant act of injustice, unworthy of the government in whose defense these men risked their lives, yet being in the government employ, were not men in uniform required to risk their lives.

THE JAWS OF DEATH

In late September of 1874, the 4th U.S. Cavalry, out of Fort Concho, Texas, was busily engaged in searching for a band of maurauding Indians who had jumped their reservation at Fort Sill, Oklahoma. Scouts reported them camped in the Palo Duro Canyon, located in the Texas Panhandle. The weather was atrocious.

Palo Duro had been a haven for the Plains Indians for years. The year 1874 had not been good to the Indians. Gone were the days of the buffalo and with them the thrill and excitement of the hunt. There had been few, if any, victories. Their food supplies were becoming in short ration and there was a marked decay in their old happy way of life. This was to be the last big battle, fought in the narrow confines, haze and obscurity of a canyon, which deprived the Indians of their single greatest weapon—mobility.

To the Indians, it seemed as though there were soldiers everywhere they turned. Food was becoming a problem. They had begun to argue bitterly amongst themselves. The rain fell almost incessantly. When the weather finally did become fair, the Indians turned toward the friendly sanctuary of Palo Duro Canyon, where they believed themselves to be safe from the pony-soldiers, being assured by the medicine man that in Palo Duro they would be safe from harm.

The troopers bivouacked for the night and then were back in the saddle again at 4:00 A.M. They arrived at the rim of the

81

gorge at daybreak. Hundreds of teepees stretched out over the canyon floor. A large herd of ponies had been put out to graze. The only trail leading into the canyon was referred to as a "goat trail," although there never had been any goats in the area. The troopers were ordered to descend the 1200-foot canyon wall into what they referred to as the "jaws of death." Leading their mounts, scrambling and skidding down the zigzagging trail, they descended in a single file. The early morning lie-abed habits and lack of organization of the Indians helped the troopers arrive on the canyon floor undetected. Had they been observed, it would have been sure death to all. Once they had attained the floor of the canyon, it would be a simple matter for the Indians to cut off their retreat, and by sheer attrition alone, every white man would surely die. However, the Indians had been taken completely by surprise.

The troopers deployed and immediately opened fire. The Indians fled helter-skelter from the surprise attack, leaving all of their personal belongings in their frantic haste to escape the troopers' fire. As the troops set about corraling the large pony herd, the Indians began to recover from the initial shock of the troopers' fire, struggling to regroup so they could return the troopers' volleys. One trooper was struck in the bowels and fell from his horse. While three troops engaged the Indians in long range carbine fire, others commenced to sack the village.

The Indians quickly gathered their large pony herd while others delivered fire from every quarter, behind each bush and behind every rock. Smoke from the rifle and pistol fire added to the eerie gloom of the canyon and mingled with the flash from the many guns.

While the Indians were being held at bay by fire from one group of troopers, another group of soldiers set out in quick pursuit of the rapidly disappearing pony herd. Capture of this herd proved to be relatively simple.

The troopers deployed in a skirmish line across the canyon floor became subject to enfilading fire from the Indians above. Here and there a horse fell, but the same miracle that

82

had gotten them down the canyon walls undetected, now protected them again. Not one trooper was hit.

When the Indians attempted to block their escape route the troopers sent a detail to rout them and then hold the trail open. One of the troops was deployed as skirmishers while the rest set to collecting the belongings of the Indians and placing them into immense heaps prior to setting them afire. Loot was scattered over a large area of the canyon floor.

By mid-afternoon, the troopers were ready to withdraw.

The Indians kept up a sporadic fire, but finally abandoned the fight altogether. Without their ponies, the Indians were beaten.

Knowing the Indians were defeated without supplies, the Army decided to withdraw about 20 miles, taking over 2000 Indian ponies with them. They knew the Indians would attempt to recapture their ponies, and also realized they would be unable to prevent it, so the animals were taken aside and shot.

All the fight went out of the Indians. Soon they began to struggle back to Fort Sill. The destruction of their ponies forced them to return to Fort Sill in disgrace—by walking. For the Indians, all trails led only to Fort Sill, and then as before, it started to rain.

No trooper had been killed and only one had been wounded. The men had been in the saddle for 34 hours, ridden over 70 miles and fought Indians for two to three hours.

Earnest Veuve, Farrier, Troop A. 4th U.S. Cavalry, "gallant manner in which he faced a desperate Indian." John W. Comfort, Corporal, Troop A, 4th U.S. Cavalry, "ran down and killed an Indian." Frederick Bergendahl, Private, Band, and John O'Sullivan, Private, Troop I, 4th U.S. Cavalry, both "gallantry in long chase after Indians."

HE CAME TO FIGHT

One cannot find the name of Captain Frank D. Baldwin on the Medal of Honor rolls for the Indian campaigns. One would have to search the rolls for those Medals awarded during the Civil War where his first Medal was awarded for the actions at Peach Tree Creek, Georgia, in 1864. Captain Baldwin was nominated the second time during the Civil War, but did not receive the second Medal at that time. He was, however, the first man to be nominated for three Medals of Honor. A group which includes only one other man.

At McClellan's Creek, Texas, on 8 November 1874, Captain Baldwin, "rescued, with two companies, two white girls, by a voluntary attack upon Indians whose superior numbers and strong position would have warranted delay for reinforcements, but which delay would have permitted the Indians to escape and kill their captives."

Captain Baldwin's command had started out from the north bank of the Red River on 4 November and after three days of hard riding, had arrived along the banks of McClellan's Creek, a fork of the Red River, east of Amarillo, Texas, and drew up in line prepatory to attack.

Included in Captain Balwin's hodge-podge command were units from the 6th Cavalry, 5th Infantry, Scouts, a mountain howitzer and 23 six-mule teams, with empty wagons. Captain Baldwin's orders had been to proceed north and east to a supply camp on the Washita, about 200 miles south of Fort Dodge. If Indians were sighted, he was to send a scout, and should contact be made, "to attack or pursue as you deem necessary."

Knowing that it would be Gray Beard and his band should contact be made, there was plenty of reason to attack, even without orders. Gray Beard was the prime suspect of holding two young white girls captive. (Story of Germain massacre.) Captain Baldwin's immediate problem was the mule teams. They could not be taken along and they could not be left behind unprotected. If men were left behind to protect the mules, there would not be enough troopers left to mount an effective attack. There was really no second choice. The teamsters, wagons and mules would have to participate in the attack.

A line was formed with the mule wagons in the center. There was an area of open ground to be crossed before the Indian camp was reached, which was located in an open space at the edge of a cottonwood grove. Before the men could get on the move, they were sighted by the Indians who gave the alarm, then prepared to make a stand. All the troopers were warned to be on the lookout for the two white girls, then Captain Baldwin shouted, "Forward ho!" and the men and wagons went careening across the plains, the infantry in the wagons, the cavalry on the flanks.

As soon as the troopers came within range, the Indians opened fire. There were at least 300 Cheyenne Dog Soldiers and they outnumbered the troopers by three to one.

With the frightened mules leading the way, the blue line moved unflinchingly forward. Here and there a horse fell, or a man went down, but they moved inexorably across the open ground.

The Indians continued their fusillade from behind any cover they could manage, but their line began to waver, then break, before such an onslaught.

By now the mule-skinners were standing in the wagon boots, driving like madmen, whips popping, wagons bouncing and clattering, mules with ears laid back, nostrils wide open and aflame, eyes rolling in their sockets, all caught up in a wild cacophony which sounded like a bunch of drunken banshees. Even the infantry and cavalry began to shout and holler in the spirit of things, adding to the din. Never before had the Indians been confronted by such a charge. With those wall-eyed lop-eared mules in the van, the Indians' resistance broke.

The wagons went hurtling into the Indian camp hell-bent, scattering Indians like a covey of quail. For a few brief moments there was a wild melee, the likes of which had never been seen before, men and animals running helter-skelter in all directions. The Indians tried one more scattered volley, then fled on pony, on foot, any way to escape these madmen, leaving behind their dead and wounded. Some of the Indians rallied to harass the troopers in a 12-mile running battle, but they broke off the fight and disappeared.

Captain Baldwin's charge had been spectacular, grand and most effective, even though it had had its ludicrous aspects. Nevertheless, Captain Baldwin had gotten the job done.

A large number of Indian ponies were captured, the Indian camp was completely destroyed, the Indian tribe disbanded, temporarily at least. Inside one of the teepees, huddled beneath a large, dirty buffalo robe, alive and unhurt, they found the two white captive girls.

LEFT, RIGHT AND CENTER

Troop H, 6th U.S. Cavalry, Sappa Creek, Kansas, 23 April 1875. Avers, James F., Private: Dawson, Michael, Trumpeter: Gardiner, Peter W., Private: Hornaday, Simpson, Private; Lowthers, James, Private; Platten, Frederick, Sergeant; Robbins, Marcus M., Private; Tea, Richard L., Sergeant; "Gallanty in Action."

During the early spring of 1875, the 6th U.S. Cavalry was stationed at Fort Lyons, Kansas. In April of that year, Sergeant Frederick Platten was ordered to mount twenty men and join Lieutenant Austin Henely at Fort Wallace. They were to become part of an expedition outfitted at Fort Dodge to pursue hostile Cheyennes in the general area of northwestern Kansas. As the first glint of sun was poking its way through a thin veil of clouds, the columns moved in a northwesterly direction toward Sappa Creek, whose two main forks join near Oberlin and flow into Nebraska southeast of McCook.

When they had proceeded to within five miles of Sappa Creek, two scouts came galloping back to the columns with the news that Indians had been located on the opposite bank of the north fork of Sappa Creek. Before daybreak the following day, the troops had moved out and headed toward the Indian encampment.

The morning was clear and cold and the prairie sod was moist and soft under the horses' hooves. As the troops neared the Indian village, it was decided to have the men close in as near as possible to the camp as could be accomplished unde-tected and then charge, using their service revolvers instead of the slower firing carbines.

Trumpeter Michael Dawson was sent on ahead alone, to inform the scouts of the main bodies' intentions. A small party headed by Sergeant George Kitchen, a Medal of Honor reci-pient at Upper Washita, Texas, in September of the previous year, was detailed to sweep up the Indian pony herd. Five men under the command of Corporal Edward Sharpless, also a Medal of Honor winner the previous year at Upper Washita, Texas, were left to guard the supply wagons. The rest of the men moved out at a smart gait directly toward the teepees, which were still obscured from view behind the hills bordering the creek.

As the men attempted to cross the Sappa at one of its many horseshoe bends, the horses started to panic when they began to mire down in the soft, slimy mud and spring float of the marshy ground bordering the creek. This delay in comple-tion of the movement for a charge, allowed the Indians time to regroup into defensive positions.

Before the entire command could free itself from the creek, the Indians were called upon to surrender.

A ragged, inaccurate volley of fire was the Indians answer to the demand. As Sergeant Platten was emerging from the water, leading his mount, an arrow struck him a glancing blow on the back of the neck, which injury was most serious to his pride. In spite of orders not to break ranks, two troopers charged the now completely encircled Indians. Both troopers paid for their rashness with their lives and both losses were wholly unnecessary. The deaths of the two troopers infuriated those remaining so that they rose to stand on the skyline, firing wild volleys and preparing to charge without orders.

The Indians began to fall like tenpins. The Army six-shooter was far superior to the Indian's bow and arrow for close fighting. Many of the Indians feigned death, however. One Indian rode into the blue ranks and an Indian lying on the ground leaped up behind him. The rescuer died for his deed from a hail of bullets, but the rescued Indian managed his escape. As the troopers prepared to advance, a hostile was noticed to make for the body of one of the two brash troopers killed earlier. It being a point of honor and respect to save him from being scalped and mutilated, Sergeant Platten was ordered to kill the Indian. Then it was noticed a second hostile was approaching. A command was given to countermand the first order, but Sergeant Platten either did not hear the second order, or chose to ignore it.

Sergeant Platten, carbine in one hand, pistol in the other, ducked an arrow unleashed by an Indian and charged. One of the Indians raised his rifle to fire and Platten killed him with one snap shot from his service revolver. The second Indian, armed only with a bow and arrow, turned heel and fled. Calmly and deliberately holstering his revolver and at a range of less than 100 yards, Sergeant Platten raised his carbine and fired. One shot was enough. The Indian leaped into the air and fell dead. Neither of these two Indians would carry any more scalps on the way to his happy hunting ground.

The fight flared and waned, then flared and waned again. Trumpeter Dawson's horse was killed by a single shot from an Indian marksman. Determined to bring the engagement to a quick and decisive decision, orders were given for a final assault. A group of men was sent to a strategic crest of a ridge. Private Marcus Robbins volunteered to lead four or five men out of sight down the creek and wade back to come in the rear of the Indian rifle pits. At a given signal, the group on the crest of the ridge began to deliver a heavy continuous fire, killing any Indian foolish enough to expose himself and compelling the living to crouch in their pits to escape sure death. The assault group rose to charge.

A few minutes of close combat and the issue was no longer in doubt. The surviving Indians died desperately.

Private Robbins, rushing up from the creek, emptied his service revolver into a hostile, which action saved the life of his "bunkie."

An Indian fired point blank at one of the scouts, the bullet striking the scout's cartridge case. The Indian ran a few paces and threw himself behind a fold in the ground to reload.

A young, hot-blooded trooper charged after the Indian, firing his revolver wildly. Clutching his empty revolver, the trooper came to an abrupt halt as the Indian thrust his reloaded weapon forward, thumb on the hammer. The scout fired and the Indian slumped forward with most of his head shot away, his thumb still on the hammer of his rifle, still at "half-cock."

The camp was ordered burned. As the troopers were busily engaged in looting, one of the Indians, a chief, who had been playing dead, charged Platten with a knife.

Private James F. Ayers killed the Indian with a well-placed shot. Sergeant Platten added the chief's magnificent war bonnet to the collection of plunder.

Shortly after the action at Sappa Creek, the 6th was sent to Arizona to fight the Apaches.

A LESSON IN MANNERS

By 1876, the war against the various tribes of the Sioux Nation had exploded over the entire frontier—from Nebraska, to Dakota, to Wyoming, to Montana. During the intervening years Patrick Leonard had swapped the yellow of the cavalry for the blue of the Infantry and was now a Corporal in Company A, 23rd U.S. Infantry Regiment, Mounted.

That wily old Sioux warrior, Red Cloud, was making war noises again. His medicine man had recounted tales of past glories and promised the young braves their chances to become heroes. The number of incidents began to increase alarmingly and in ferocity; pillaging, looting, burning homesteads, ambushing stagecoaches and stealing cattle. The more the Indians saw they could get away with the bolder they became.

Finally, with the War Department's patience exhausted, the 23rd was ordered to teach the Indians a lesson on how they should behave. Only a small few thought that teaching the Indians how to behave would prove to be difficult.

As a frontier regiment, the 23rd was pretty green. Outside of a scattering of veterans like Corporal Leonard, most of the men were fresh from the East, with little or no experience in fighting Indians.

A Sioux Indian prisoner, brought to Fort Hartsuff, Nebraska, told of a large Indian raiding party of about 200 braves, whose teepees were set up some fifteen miles away.

The inexperienced and anxious officers of the 23rd decided this was as good an opportunity as any to start teaching the Indians lessons in manners. Three companies of the 32rd were ordered to fall out in full battle dress, find the Indians and deliver their first lesson. It was a little past noon by the time everyone was ready and the columns swung out the gates of the fort and headed in the direction of the suspected Sioux camp. Because they had gotten such a late start, it was calculated the entire distance to the Indian camp could not be traversed in one afternoon. After a short march, bivouac was prepared for the night.

Bright and early the next morning, April 27th, while the sky was still gray with the dawn of a new day, the march was resumed at a brisk pace. It was somewhere along toward high noon that the scouts reported they had located the Indian camp. Since lesson teaching was to be the order of the day, it was decided the quicker the 23rd got started, the better. A full-scale charge on horseback by all three companies was decided upon, rather than the slower, but much safer probing foot patrols. So with bugles blaring, guidons streaming in the wind, off the 23rd rode with thundering of hooves and a cloud of dust, bent on becoming the best lesson teachers the army had. The green rookies from the East were enjoying every minute of the excitement of the charge immensely.

However, as the pulsating blue line drew closer and closer to the Indian wickiups, the old timers like Cpl. Leonard began to like it less and less. Something just didn't seem right.

It had all started out to be just another fight with some Indians. It had all started out to be just another charge, executed like at school on the parade grounds and the Indians would be routed—or so some thought. Suddenly and without any warning, withering volley upon withering volley of rifle fire enfiladed and raked the ragged blue line from the flanks. A trap, and neatly set, and the 23rd rode right into it. All around Cpl. Leonard men were lunging, sliding and falling from their saddles, like wheat before the farmer's scythe under the galling fire being set up by the Indians. There was a damn sight more than the 200 Indians here than the prisoner had said there was. A hail of Indian lead continued to cut gaping holtes in the ranks of the blue line.

First it was like a spark, then like a flame, then like a holocaust. Military cohesion began to falter, then wane, then utter panic gripped the inexperienced troops. When a man tried to rein in his mount, he only succeeded in making the fear-crazed animal rear up, blocking the way for those in the rear, or causing himself to become unseated when he could not control the wildly plunging beast. Others tried to turn and run, cutting across the path of those who followed. Utter chaos ensued!

In the midst of this seemingly total confusion, were men such as Corporal Leonard. He seemed to be everywhere at once. Slowly, ever so slowly, he got the men who had gone ashen-faced with fear from the devastating fire of the Indians, back into action and forming some sort of a line.

It was here that Cpl. Leonard set an example for the young men to follow, as he rode out in front of the line to a young comrade-in-arms, who had been horribly wounded and thrown from his horse. He now lay face down on the ground, subject to a horrendous fire from the Indians. Without a moment's hesitation, Cpl. Leonard dismounted his horse and stood astride the fallen soldier, all the while he delivered a deadly pistol fire to keep the Indians at a distance. Bellowing at some of the older men who were close at hand, Cpl. Leonard told them to come and carry the wounded and profusely bleeding trooper to safety. He continued to deliver covering fire, keeping any and all over-zealous Indians from counting new coups. When all were returned to safety, Cpl. Leonard remounted his horse and returned to the shattered line.

The charge had been a complete and total failure. But it could have been worse. It could have spelled total annihilation. As it turned out, the Sioux won the fight handily. The lesson teaching would have to come another day, but another day there would be.

Because of such men as Corporal Patrick Leonard, many of the unblooded rookies of the 23rd lived to fight again. In time. A Company of the 23rd vindicated itself and posted a brilliant record—including the final defeat of the crafty Red Cloud himself.

Patrick Leonard's second citation for the Medal of Honor reads "Gallantry in charge on hostile Sioux."

Second Lieutenant Charles H. Heyl and Corporal Jeptha L. Lytton were also awarded Medals of Honor for their deeds during this action.

THE STORY OF A BATTLE

First Sergeant Michael A. McGann, Troop F, 3rd U.S. Cavalry, "Gallantry in action." First Sergeant Joseph Robinson, Troop D, 3rd U.S. Cavalry, "Discharged his duties while in charge of the skirmish line under fire with judgement and great coolness and brought up the lead horses at a critical moment." First Sergeant John H. Shingle, Troop I, 3rd U.S. Cavalry, "Gallantry in action." Trumpeter Elmer A. Snow, Troop M, 3rd U.S. Cavalry, "Bravery in action, was wounded in both arms."

In June of 1876, General Crook was in the field to scout the country from the Powder and Tongue Rivers north to the Yellowstone River and cooperate with Generals Terry and Gibbon. Fresh Indian signs indicated a large party of Sioux were on the move. General Crook's intentions were to cut them off along the Rosebud River. While the men were unsaddling for a rest, the whole range of hills to their front became alive with Indians. The order was quickly passed to saddle up, expecting a battle. One troop was placed on the left flank, two troops were detailed as skirmishers and ordered to make a flank movement to the left to gain the hills.

In the attack upon the bluff, the troops suffered severely, expecially Troop L. Captain Henry of D Troop brought up reinforcements which prevented Troop L from being cut off and chopped to pieces. In the ensuing melee, Captain Henry was shot through the face. With blood gushing from his mouth, the gallant officer fell from his horse.

At this time, General Crook, who was stationed on one of the hills near the center of the line where he could view all that was taking place, wished to send an order to an officer on one of the other hills. He directed his orderly, Trumpeter Snow, to carry it with all haste.

The most direct route for Trumpeter Snow was down the steep side of one hill and then up the steep side of the other. The chances of his reaching his destination alive appeared slim. Trumpeter Snow, on as fast a horse as could be found, took the most direct route, hotly chased by two Indians. The two Indians, seeing they would be unable to overtake Snow's swift mount, began firing their rifles at him. Their marksmanship proved to be quite excellent as Trumper Snow fell heavily from his horse, horribly and painfully shot through both arms. Trumpeter Snow struggled valiantly to his feet, and under the protection of his comrades' intense and accurate covering fire, delivered his urgent and blood-soaked message.

Now the Indians charged en masse. It looked as though the men were doomed. The Indians pressed forward, not once flinching from the searing fire of the troopers, which was cutting gaping holes in their ranks.

When the hostilites had first commenced, First Sergeant Shingle was placed in command of the horses of four dismounted troops by Captain Henry, and when the officer fell, Sgt. Shingle saw the men waver slightly. Leaving the horses in charge of another trooper, he leaped aboard and rushed into the thickest of the fight. He performed exceedingly valuable service in rallying the breaking ranks, which enabled the hard-pressed troops to hold the Indians at bay. The sergeant's voice could be heard loud and clear above the tumult, "Face them men, face them."

The line fired into the Indians at such short range as to almost burn the noses of the Indian ponies with the flash from gun muzzles.

The Indians were driven back 200 yards over the slope on the troopers' front, where support troops put the redskins to rout. Those Indians left alive headed for the valley of the Little Big Horn River to join their allies.

A FEW GOOD MEN

Gold had been discovered in the Black Hills of the Great Sioux Reservation, Dakota Territory, in 1874. By year's end 1875, the War Department issued a directive which ordered all Indians in the Black Hills on to reservations by the end of January 1876, or else they would be treated as hostiles. Several sharp and bloody engagements were fought during March, May and early June 1876. The War Department, incensed at the Indians' behavior, and badgered by political big-wigs, gave General Phillip H. Sheridan orders to launch a spirited attack against the hostiles during the summer of 1876. General Sheridan then placed General Alfred H. Terry in charge of a great field campaign designed to entrap the hostiles in a three-pronged pincers movement.

General Terry and his command were to form one prong of the pincers movement. The largest part of General Terry's command consisted of the entire 7th U.S. Cavalry Regiment, stationed at Fort Abraham Lincoln, Bismarck, Dakota Territory. The 7th was marched rapidly to the valley of the Little Big Horn River, arriving there on June 25th. Executing a highly controversial maneuver, the 7th was divided into four groups. The first group was assigned the task of attacking an immense Indian encampment located on the valley floor, at its southernmost end. The second group was designated to guard the pack train. The third group was ordered to scout the regiment's left flank. The fourth group would attempt a flanking maneuver against the Indian villages.

When the first group attacked the southern end of the Indian villages, the overwhelming number of Indians forced this group to quickly retreat to a defensive position on some high bluffs of land overlooking the Little Big Horn River. Late during the afternoon of June 25th, the first group was joined by the second and also by the third group. These three groups now became one cohesive, defensive force, entrenched on the high bluffs of land overlooking the river. Unbeknown to the force on the bluffs, the hostile Indian warriors were overwhelming and annihilating to a man, the fourth group, containing their comrades-in-arms, five miles to the north.

The force on the high bluffs overlooking the river had suffered heavy casualties during the earlier fighting. Due to the hot and sultry weather at that time of the year, water soon became in short supply. It appeared next to impossible for any of the encircled troopers to break free from the band of warriors surrounding their position and the Indians seemed reluctant to close in to try and finish the job. The excitement of the battle and the heat of the day made their thirst almost maddening. Tobacco in any form was forbidden. Some of the troopers put pebbles in their mouths to try to excite the glands, while some ate grass roots, but none could find relief from the terrible thirst. When attempts were made to eat hard bread, it was only a matter of moments before it was blown out of the mouth like so much flour. The scorching sun continued to beat down incessantly to a point, where men even found it difficult to swallow.

By mid-day June 26th, the wounded were by now in desperate need of water. The only surving surgeon notified the officer in charge that unless several of the more severely wounded were given water—and soon—many would die.

Volunteers were immediately called upon to make a sortie to the river in an attempt to procure the much-needed water. Water! But how was it to be obtained? Here they were, situated on the steep bluffs several hundred feet above the surging current of the river and as far as any of them knew, every foot of that distance was under the watchful eye of a cunning foe.

The moaning of the sorely stricken wounded was interrupted by incessant calls for water. The shrieks of the wounded rang out on all sides. Tears came to the men's eyes when they heard the poor devils moaning with pain. Nothing else was thought of but answering those piteous calls.

Making a particularly dangerous reconnaissance, one particular ravine, of the many ravines in the area, appeared to be completely devoid of Indians and also appeared to be quite free from Indian rifle fire. It was noted this ravine would provide adequate concealment almost all the way to the river's edge. Each man came carrying as many canteens as he thought he could manage and someone had an inspiration and came forth with an old camp kettle.

To provide the men who were going to venture to the river with as much protection as possible, four men, Sergeant George H. Geiger, Saddler Otto Voit, Blacksmith Henry W. B. Mechlin and Private Charles Windolph, did, as their citations read, "With three comrades during the entire engagement, courageously held a position that secured water for the command." These four men advanced to a high point of land well outside the defense perimeter. Then, standing erect in full view of all, both white man and Indian alike, they fired their carbines to draw attention and fire to themselves and away from the water carriers. The point of land upon which these four men stood is now called Medal of Honor Point and is a part of the Reno-Benteen Battlefield, Custer Battlefield National Monument, Crow Agency, Montana.

The party of water volunteers consisted entirely of enlisted men and no one seemed to really be in command unless it was Mike Madden, Saddler, who shouted in his thick Irish brogue, "Come on, fellers, lave us run."

The rush to the head of the ravine was made in safety by all but Private Campbell, who, scant feet short of the shelter of the head of the ravine, was felled by a rifle bullet in the shoulder. Campbell stopped, looked at his shattered shoulder with a foolish smile on his face and crumpled in a heap. Some of the men halted immediately to offer him assistance, but in a personal agony which made him writhe with pain, he told them pluckily to "go on, boys I can make it back some way."

Once they entered the shelter of the ravine, which was very deep and crooked, the troopers instinctively strung out in skirmish-type formation, every man on the alert, carbines held at the ready, Madden in the lead. Slowly, ever so slowly, cautiously ever so cautious, scouting every turn in the tortuous ravine, they moved closer and closer to the river's edge. Finally, they reached the bottom of the ravine without encountering any Indians or seeing any signs, save an occasional pony track.

The exact number of men who participated in the *journada* to the river for water has never been determined; however, fifteen men did receive Medals of Honor for the efforts. They were Private Neil Bancroft; Private Abraham B. Brant; Private Thomas J. Callan; Private Theodore W. Goldin; Private David W. Harris; Private William M. Harris (not related); Sergeant Rufus D. Hutchinson; Sergeant Stanislaus Roy; Private James Pym; Private George D. Scott; Private Thomas W. Stevens (Stivers); Private Peter Thompson; Private Frank Tolan; Private Frederick Deitline; and Private Charles H. Welch. Armed with canteens and the camp kettle and under the protective fire from the sharpshooters, these heroic men made their way to the bottom of the ravine.

Once they had reached the bottom of the ravine, the men noted the sides of the ravine protected them from sight and from rifle fire, save but from directly across the river. They could see many Indians moving about, but it was evident they had not as yet been detected. During a hurried council, it was decided the best plan would be to take the camp kettle, dash the few remaining yards to the river, fill it, get back under cover as quickly as possible, and then transfer the precious fluid to the canteens. Two-by-two they took turns at the hazardous work. Much to their surprise, not a single shot was fired in their direction. The desperate need for water by wounded comrades made haste imperative. It took but a few short minutes to fill the canteens. After a steep climb up the hill, the water was turned over to those in charge. The cool liquid was placed to the lips of the wounded.

One bandaged trooper refused to drink. He was a tall, good-looking fellow with a bloody rag wrapped around his head, who pointed to a wounded comrade and said, "He needs it more."

Later in the day, due to the dire need for water, it was determined to try the same feat again. The first party assembled to a man—with possibly some additions. A rush was made to the ravine as before, and a less cautious, more emboldened advance was carried out to the river's edge. The hidden camp kettle was once again brought into play, duplicating the tactics which had proven so successful the first time.

It was Madden's decision to return back up the hill with the camp kettle filled full of water, also. Madden and Dwyer, who had been partners before, grabbed the kettle and were off. Having successfully filled the camp kettle with water, the return dash for safety was made. They were almost within the safety of the ravine when a withering volley of rifle fire from the bushes on the opposite side of the river stormed into them and Madden went down, shot through the leg, shattering the bone.

Dwyer was unhit, but the old camp kettle had not fared so well. It would never be the same again, as it spouted water from a half a dozen bullet holes. Heavy fire was returned by the troopers but no more shots came from the hostiles. Now they were not only confronted with the problem of getting the precious water up the hill, but also Madden.

Madden suggested he be left behind with his carbine, but this suggestion was turned down unanimously. After a brief conference between the others, two of the men grabbed Madden. Mercifully for him, he passed out and was thereby spared the agonizing pain of the return journey up the steep trail. Although Madden's bearers had to be changed frequently, the hospital area was finally achieved. Madden's leg had to be amputated above the knee—without an anesthetic.

For personal and outstanding heroism, Sergeant Benjamin C. Criswell; Sergeant Richard P. Hanley; Private Charles Cunningham; Private Henry Holden; and Sergeant Thomas Murry were also awarded Medals of Honor. Sergeant Criswell recovered the body of an officer from within the Indian lines, brought up ammunition and encouraged the men, while in the most exposed conditions. Sergeant Hanley recaptured a stampeded mule, loaded with ammunition, singlehanded without orders, from within the enemy lines, under a galling fire from the Indians which lasted a full five minutes. Private Cunningham refused to leave the firing line although wounded in the neck and in an extremely exposed position. He fought bravely throughout the day. Private Holden brought up ammunition under a most galling fire. Sergeant Murry brought up the pack train and rations under fire from the Indians.

There were many others who performed bravely, but whose deeds went unrewarded. Private Edward Davern, whose horse had been killed in a hand-to-hand fight with an Indian, shot the Indian dead, caught the Indian's pony, and rode it to his command. Private William George, being horribly shot, and suffering terribly, asked for something to relieve the pain and when told there was nothing available, uttered not another word of complaint. He later died. Private Patrick M. Golden, having survived the fighting on June 25th, told a bunkie that if the Indians came back on the 26th, he would be killed. When the Indians opened the hostilities during the morning's gray dawn, the first Indian volley to hit the troopers' line, struck Golden in the head, and he was instantly killed. Private Henry Klotzboucher, mortally wounded during the initial assault, was dragged into a clump of trees and left with a canteen of water. He was later found dead. Corporal George Lell was fatally wounded on June 26th. Knowing that death was near, he requested to be lifted up to see the faces of the men once more before he died. Held up in a sitting position, he died with a smile on his face. Private Charles Sanders sat on the firing line, laughing and cursing at what poor shots the Indians were because they could not hit him. Private James Severs chased a loaded mule into the Indian lines, and returned with it, unharmed. Sergeant Charles White, though badly wounded, having been shot through the elbow, gave each man a spoonful of jelly he had in his saddlebags.

These men were tried and pressed as few men had been tried and pressed before. Men fell in crumpled heaps. Men bled and died. Men threw up their arms and collapsed, never to rise again.

Theodore Golden later remarked that a survey of the water carriers, showed that none could have done less than he did, and retained his self-respect. Lying in that hospital area were wounded comrades, bunkies and friends, with whom they had fought. These men were calling piteously for water, and any man who would not have taken such risks was unworthy to wear the uniform of a soldier.

A SHORT TRIP TO HELL

After the defeat of Custer and the successful retreat of the Sioux and Cheyenne, the government quickly ordered reinforcements into the field. It was not, however, until nearly a year later, until after the Indians had met with several crushing defeats, had been pursued until they were utterly exhausted, that peace was declared. These defeats administered to the Indians were by the Third, Fourth and Fifth Cavalries. With a terrible persistence, these tattered soldiers clung to the Indian trails with a resolution and determination that nothing could shake and entitles them to the respect and admiration of their countrymen.

Many a long and hard march was made on the trail of the Indians. Under burning suns, suns which parched the ground as bare as the palm of the hand. Through torrents of drenching rains. Through snows and cold of unexampled severity. The trooper's ration became so short he was forced to subsist on mule meat and wild onions.

Then by 7 September 1876, one command found it had reached the end of its resources and the limit of its endurance.

But the Indians were in a bad way too. Although they were worn thin and near exhaustion by the energetic and ruthless pursuit of the troopers, they had plenty to eat.

One hundred and fifty of the soldiers who showed the fewest signs of the hardships they had endured in their pursuit of the Indians were sent to Deadwood City in the Black Hills of South Dakota to get "Any kind of provisions, for God's sake!" They were not expected to hunt for, or to fight Indians, primarily that is. They were to go for food.

As they marched southward, scouts located a large Indian village of about 50 lodges at a place called Slim Buttes, in the northwest corner of South Dakota. The camp was located on a small rising from the banks of a tiny stream called Rabbit Creek. The place was enclosed on three sides by a series of tall cliffs, whose broken sides seemed here and there to have been cut in half-formed terraces making an ascent easy. Little ravines and small canyons ran through the buttes, gradually climbing until they met the plateau on top.

The troopers instantly determined to attack the camp. Troop disposition was made with care. The troops halted in a deep gorge on the night of 8 September, preparing to do battle early the next morning. The night was dark, cold, and quite rainy and the tired men suffered greatly. Marching out at dawn, the troopers succeeded in surprising the Indian camp. Twenty-five mounted men charged directly into the Indian camp. The remaining men dismounted, formed two parties and advanced on the Indian village from two separate sides.

The attack was a complete success. The village was taken with but little loss. Some of the Sioux were driven into one of the canyons which ended in a cave. Being in complete command of the village the entire command was ordered to gather together. To their joy, they found ample provisions of food for both men and animals. However, there still remained the little band of savages in the ravine to be dealt with. A detachment was ordered to drive them out.

The Indians had not wasted their time. They had busied themselves digging rifle pits and as the soldiers advanced to storm the cave, they were met by a rapid and well-directed fire. Two of the troopers were shot dead and several others wounded. The Indians' position seemed impregnable. An interpreter crept up and called upon the Indians to surrender.

The Indians replied with taunts and jeers and informed him that Crazy Horse was in the vicinity and would undoub-

108

tedly come to their rescuc when he heard of their plight. Meanwhile, the survivors of the village, perhaps as many as one hundred warriors, formed an extended line on the buttes and opened fire on the soldiers.

Reinforcements for the besieged troopers were sent for at once. Then preparations were quickly made to hold the provisions that had been captured, to deny them to the Indians. At the same time they continued to prosecute the attack against the Indians still secreted in the cave, while all the time keeping up a smart fight with the Indians on the buttes. About mid-day the reinforcements arrived.

The men immediately moved forward under a galling fire to dislodge the Indians in the cave. Once again the Indians were offered surrender terms. Once again they refused. The men opened fire and searched every nook and cranny of the cave with a hail of bullets. After two hours of firing, the Indians were again called upon to surrender. This time the request met some response.

Thirteen squaws and children came forward. Most of the braves refused to give up, still confident that Crazy Horse would soon succor them. The offer of mercy was made a fourth time. A young Indian and another young warrior stepped forward, supporting their chief, who had been shot horribly through the bowels. He was suffering frightfully, but controlled himself as he surrendered his rifle. Everything possible was done medically but the wound was beyond human skill.

Inside the cave, the rocky walls were cut and scored by the rain of bullets poured into it by the troopers.

Too late, Crazy Horse, with some six-hundred braves, appeared on the scene. Thinking he had only to deal with a small force, he galloped gallantly forward to the attack around five o'clock in the afternoon. He retired quickly to the top of the buttes and the soldiers dashed after him. By the time the troopers reached the level of the plateau, Crazy Horse had wisely departed having sustained some small loss.

It was one of the most picturesque battles ever fought in the West. The officers had stood in the center of a vast ampitheater, ringed by hostile fire, and issued orders directing the troopers' volleys.

Sergeant John A. Kirkwood and Private Robert Smith "gallantly endeavored to dislodge some Sioux secreted in a ravine."

A YANKEE DOODLE DANDY

     Colonel Ranald S. McKenzie led his own regiment, the Fourth Cavalry, plus troops from the Second, Third and Fifth Cavalries, the Ninth, Fourteenth and Twenty-Third Infantries, four batteries of the Fourth Artillery, 400 Indian scouts, 168 wagons, 7 ambulance and 400 pack mules, into the Big Horn Mountains toward the canyon of Crazy Woman's Fork of the Powder River, where Dull Knife's Cheyenne village was located.

     Steadily, but cautiously, the troops forged ahead. By nightfall of 25 November 1876, they were close enough to hear the dance drums of Dull Knife's Cheyennes, throbbing, throbbing, throbbing. The troops went into hiding during the frigid night. At dawn, the unsuspected attack was a complete surprise. The fight raged back and forth through the village, back and forth along the canyon, up and down its sides. The troops, having learned many a bitter lesson, quickly put the torch to the Indian supplies.

     The Indians battled back once more from a cliff top, opened a murderous fire on the troops below.

     The troops stormed the heights from all sides, putting the Indians into a pell-mell rout. This was the beginning of the end for the Cheyennes, when they lost the battle in the canyon. The army had no intention of letting go.

     First Sergeant Thomas H. Forseyth, "though dangerously wounded, he maintained his ground with a small party against a largely superior force after his commanding officer had been shot down during a sudden attack and rescued that officer and a comrade from the enemy.''

A SALUTE TO GLORY

Three times in the history of American arms, an entire command has been wiped out. All three occurred during the Indian campaigns and all three were by Sioux Indians. (Gratton—Feterman—Custer). In what was then Montana Territory in 1876, the mighty Sioux and the bloodthirsty Cheyennes had joined forces. The troopers had burned out the Cheyennes at what is known as the Dull Knife Raid the year before. The Cheyennes had then turned to their age-old enemies, the Sioux, for help. Having suffered heavily from the white soldiers, eager to gain fighting warriors, Sitting Bull and Crazy Horse had lent a generous hand.

Once more whipped into a screaming frenzy by a medicine man, these war-painted braves rode the length and breadth of their land with but a single thought in mind, kill all of the white men, burn their homes, wipe them forever from the lands that, since time immemorial, had belonged to the red man. The great Sioux chieftain, Sitting Bull, now held sway over 8000 blood lusting, kill-crazy braves. Now there was going to be Hell to pay!

It was decided the only way to make this country tenable for whites was to make it untenable for the Indians. As soon as he had received orders to occupy this countrty, General Nelson A. Miles immediately mapped plans for a strong winter campaign. General Miles' experience had taught him that the only way and logical time to fight the Indians was during the winter months when he was unable to move great distances.

The Army had always felt the Powder River country, with its intense cold and deep snows was impossible for white men to winter in except in well prepared shelters.

General Miles contended that if the Indian could live in this country in the winter in skin teepees, the white man, with his superior appliances could not only exist here in the winter, but could move about in any circumstances, something the Indian could only do with the greatest of difficulty.

The main obstacle standing in the Indians' path to glory was the thin blue line of the Fifth and Twenty-Second Infantry Regiments, on duty west of the Missouri River. They were ordered north, past the Yellowstone River, to carry on a vigorous campaign against one of the two most troublesome tribes of Indians on the North American continent—the Sioux. The Army was going to try a new tactic to wear down the Indians and force their submission. During the winter months, the Indian would be kept on the move, not allowing him to get set or allow him any rest.

For many years, the military had interdicted the Indians' source of supply. Food and clothing were both in short supply for the Indians and now he was to be denied any rest to rebuild his commissary. Strategically the Indian was beaten, but tactically he was not quite ready to give up. This was going to be a long campaign with many battles.

As was the Army's way to identify an action, skirmish, engagement, battle, or campaign, they most often chose either the nearest water or large land mass, as a means of identification and general location. This particular campaign encompassed 21 October 1876 to 8 January 1877. Some of the more notable fights during the Cedar Creek Campaign were the Battle of the Butte and Wolf Mountain. It became known as the Cedar Creek campaign because contact with the Indians was first made on 21 October 1876 along the banks of Cedar Creek and ended with the battle of Wolf Mountain on 8 January 1877.

The troops left their cantonment at the mouth of the Tongue River on 29 December 1876, anxious to bring to a speedy conclusion a long and so far highly successful campaign. The troops started out in very inclement weather. The thermometer registered at thirty degrees below zero and in shaded pockets, the snow was a foot deep. However, thanks to General Miles' foresight, the troops were well equipped for such weather. Food and warm clothing, for both men and animals, was abundantly supplied.

The main body of Indians had been retreating up the valley of the Tongue River. On the 3rd of January 1877, a sharp clash was fought along the banks of the Tongue. By 6th January, the command had penetrated the enemy's country for a distance of some 115 miles. They went into camp near a grove of trees. As the troops were preparing breakfast on 7 January, they looked up to see Indians occupying the high ground to their right. The area was dominated by Battle Butte.

A gaudily painted Indian carrying many scalps, brought a simple and short message. "Get out or die."

Then without a word, the Indian wheeled his prancing, high-spirited, magnificently ornamented pony and rode back out of sight. Resplendent in a magnificent war bonnet, resplendent in his primitive grace, with head held high and his back ramrod straight, he rode out of sight without so much as a backward glance.

As the Indian disappeared from view behind a rise in the ground, a grayish-black colored line was seen to form on the horizon which appeared to be moving forward. Suddenly the line turned to a bright red-orange in color, looming dark and ominous. As the breeze freshened, a hot wave was wafted to the faces of the troopers. FIRE! Panic began to supplement military discipline. Company G, 5th Infantry, held the right flank of the regimental line and was most directly in the path of the now rapidly approaching flames.

Out country has a proud heritage of individual courage and bravery. To those who set duty before self, in our faith, a higher honor mortal man cannot give. As in many battles, it is the quality of leadership which turns the tide of battle and is, therefore, the deciding quality.

Sergeant Henry Hogan was Irish-born. He had always loved a good fight. He had met and fought the Indians for six years, from Nebraska westward. He had fought them in head-on charges, ambushes, night raids, rescue parties and picket duty. In the rain, in the snow, in the mountains and on the prairie. He had managed to keep his scalp intact, but never had he encountered fire before.

The green shavetail commanding Company G went ashen-faced and ordered the troops to fall back to the protection of some trees a few hundred yards to their rear.

Sgt. Hogan frantically tried to inform the Lieutenant that if the men retreated to the seeming protection of the trees, they would surely all be roasted alive. The lieutenant sat his horse with a blank look on his face, as though he were hypnotized.

Sgt. Hogan could see that he was not in a fit condition to command troops at that moment. Sgt. Hogan began to shout orders, "Get the horses through firs,t then the wagons, Be careful on the other side."

Spurring his mount forward into a dead gallop, Sgt. Hogan disappeared into the sea of flames. All along the line, men began to follow Sgt. Hogan's leadership. Company after company plunged into the flames. In a matter of moments, the flames had passed, leaving the line unharmed and intact. Sgt. Hogan had simply realized that in the strong wind, the dry grass would burn fast and the flames would remain a thin line.

But the fight was far from over. As the troops emerged from the flames, they were met by a veritable sheet of lead from the Indians' line. A charge was to be undertaken immediately to overrun the high ground upon which the Indians were located. Crazy Horse let the soldiers come, confident of victory.

Had the Indians paid any particular attention to the wagon train, they certainly would not have given second thought to two particular schooners, interspersed in the strung-out wagon train. Now out of the train swung those two wagons. Tops

116

were quickly stripped away, revealing two field pieces. The guns were quickly loaded and the muzzles elevated. Shells went screeching on their way to burst against the cliff tops.

In terror, the Sioux were close to flight, but the fighting spirit of their great war chief, Crazy Horse, kept them together.

A charge toward the key bluff on the left went on while the carbines rattled away and the artillery continued to boom. The men pushed forward, hampered by the most difficult of conditions. They dare not discard their heavy coats in the bitter cold. They struggled through the deep snow, up the steep sides of the cliffs, then made the charge in a walk.

The Indians, notoriously poor shots, in shooting downhill, constantly overshot the troopers. Then it was hand-to-hand at the crest. The whole red line began to weaken, then collapse and finally give way. Carbine fire followed them down the valley until they disappeared into a snowstorm.

Heavy clothing, deep snows and steep and slippery hillsides had made things a nightmare, but this proved to the Indians the white soldier could move about in his area, regardless of conditions.

The Indian now realized he could be hunted no matter where or when he took refuge. The Indian no longer had access to white traders, so it was impossible for him to procure arms and ammunition. The Indians realized there would be no rest or peace until they surrendered and returned to their reservations.

As one of the chiefs summed up the situation, "We are weak, compared with you and your forces; we are out of ammunition; we cannot make a rifle, a round of ammunition, or a knife; in fact, we are at an end."

Sergeant Hogan received his first Medal of Honor during the Cedar Creek campaign, along with 33 others. This total is the greatest amount of Medals of Honor awarded during the Indian Campaigns.

Those honored for the Cedar Creek Campaign along with Sgt. Hogan were: Musician John Baker; Private Richard

Burke; Sergeant Denis Byrne; Private Joseph A Cable; Private James S. Calvert; Sergeant Aquillo Coonrod; Private John S. Donelly; Private Christopher Freemeyer; Corporal John Haddoo; Corporal David Holland; Private Fred O. Hunt; Corporal Edward Johnston; Private Phillip Kennedy; First Sergeant Wendeling Kresher; Private Bernard McCann; Private Michael McCormick; Private Owen McGar; Private John McHugh; Sergeant Michael McLaughlin; Sergeant Robert McPhelan; Corporal George Miller; Private Charles Montrose; First Sergeant David Roone; Private Henry Rodenburg; Private Edward Rooney; Private David Ryan; Private Charles Sheppard; Private Patton G. Whitehead; Sergeant William Wallace; and Corporal Charles Wilson.

At Wolf Mountain, Captain James S. Casey "led his command in a successful charge against superior numbers of the enemy strongly posted." Captain Edmond Butler, "most distinguished gallantry in action with hostile Indians." First Lieutenant Robert McDonald "led his command in a successful charge against superior numbers of hostile Indians, strongly posted."

THOSE GALLANT HOURS

After Sitting Bull had been beaten at Cedar Creek, Crazy Horse defeated at Wolf Mountain, there remained then in the field but one band of sixty lodges (each lodge from five to ten persons), under Lame Deer, who positively refused to surrender. The soldiers pursued this band, overtook it, surprised it one morning in May, captured the village, dispersed the greater portion of the Indians, succeeded in isolating Lame Deer and a half dozen principal warriors.

The soldiers desired to take these Indians alive. A small body of troopers advanced toward the little group of Indians, making peace signs and uttering peace words.

The Indian, although trapped, remained extra cautious, but committed no act of hostility. The Indians came forward reluctantly, with hands extended. All seemed to be going well. It was at this point that a white scout, not knowing what was happening, dashed up and covered Lame Deer with his rifle.

Lame Deer, thinking he was to be killed, resolved to die fighting. Lifting his rifle, he pointed it straight at an officer. Just as the Indian squeezed the trigger, the officer spurred his horse causing the animal to swerve sideways. Lame Deer's bullet missed the officer by scant inches, but struck the officer's orderly full in the chest and killed him instantly. The other Indians, attempting to emulate their chief, were quickly overwhelmed by a volley of rapid carbine fire, which stretched them all dead upon the ground.

119

The troopers lost 4 killed and 7 wounded; the Indians lost 14 of their band.

Their band being broken, most of the other Indians surrendered meekly thereafter. Medals were awarded to Private William Leonard, Private Samuel D. Phillips, Corporal Harry Garland, Farrier William H. Jones, and First Sergeant Henry Wilkens, all from Troop L. 2nd U.S. Cavalry for their "gallantry in action" at Little Muddy Creek, Montana, 7 May 1877.

COUNT THE COST

Came the dawn on June 17th, 1877, the walls of Whitebird Canyon, Idaho, echoed and re-echoed to the sound of gunfire; the agonized screams of man and animals and the warwhoops of Indians.

Whitebird Creek flows through Whitebird Canyon. At its mouth, the creek flows into the Salmon River. About a mile from the Salmon, Whitebird Canyon opens out and the hills to the north swing away in a wide semi-circle, coming back to the creek where it enters the Salmon. The hills to the south rise abruptly from the banks of the creek. The floor of this one-half saucer-like valley is rolling and cut by ravines. In 1877, the valley floor had scattered stands of timber with brush in the ravines.

Late during the afternoon of June 15, Troops H and F of the 1st Cavalry, left Fort Lapwai after some Nez Percé Indians suspected of killing white settlers. A number of settlers in the area informed the officer in charge of the detail that the Indians they were probably seeking had been camped in Whitebird Canyon, about 17 miles to the southwest. A night march was undertaken with a surprise attack contemplated on the Indians just at dawn on June 17. At 1:30 A.M., the troops arrived at the head of the trail leading down into the Canyon. A halt was called until dawn so the troops could attack during daylight. The horses were unsaddled and the men instructed not to talk or use smoking tobacco.

121

As the gray of dawn tipped the western walls of the canyon, the column began moving down the steep winding trail, which took them through a narrow defile, crossing and recrossing a dry creek bed. As the column moved forward, the urge to smoke overcame one trooper and he struck a match to light his pipe. The howl of a coyote was heard at once with the call being repeated from hilltop to hilltop. As they neared the bottom of the trail the daylight began to grow brighter and the canyon was observed to open into a broad valley of several hundred acres, with deep ravines leading into the valley here and there. To the immediate front of the troops, two ridges stretched across the plateau with a shallow valley between the two ridges. To their left was a small knoll which, it was noted, occupied a very commanding position.

A small patrol was sent forward to the further of the two ridges with firm orders to send a messenger back if any Indians were observed. A group of civilian volunteers was dispatched to occupy the small knoll where they were to prevent the troops from being flanked on the left. As the detail of troopers reached the second ridge, they were seen to halt and then a lone trooper wheeled his horse and returned hell-bent for leather. Scarcely had he made his report when heavy fire was directed against those on the far ridge from behind rock, behind tree and behind bush. As troopers began to fall here and there, the rest of the command began to surge forward, willing and eager to give assistance to their sorely pressed comrades.

Down across the valley and up the slope they thundered. Reaching the crest of the second ridge, the troopers quickly dismounted and the horse holders were sent back below the ridge with the mounts. The men assumed the prone position and began returning the Indians' fire, firing at will, searching the rocks and ravines with a withering transition fire for an invisible foe. Unable to see their enemy, many of the troopers fell to the Indian rifle fire. Several of the horses, wild-eyed and with ears laid back, crazed by the almost continous boom and roar of weapons, broke loose and galloped madly about.

It was at this precise moment that a group of mounted braves, firing their rifles from beneath the necks of their galloping ponies, charged the group of brave, loyal, but inexperienced civilians on the knoll.

An alarming large number of the civilians on the knoll became incapacitated to fight and the rest fled in a frenzied panic, leaving the troopers' line exposed to Indian sharpshooters from the left and rear. Seeing the civilians fleeing the scene and suddenly receiving rifle fire from their rear, many of the troopers, most of whom were raw recruits, became infected with panic and made a rush for the horses. A scene of wild confusion ensued as the men scrambled to set their mounts. The Indians increased their fire to a crescendo and it was at this point that many of the troopers were hit. The shouts, the curses, the shrieks, and the cries of wounded men, the sound of horses screaming in agony and fear, added to the almost total confusion. Officers yelled, cursed, pleaded for the men to stand fast, to form a line and fight like men, but panic-stricken soldiers had but one thought in mind—to flee from this nightmare of deadly fire.

Finally Lieutenant Parnell succeeded in holding some of the men and they began to return the Indians' fire, stopping their seemingly overwhelming rush—temporarily, at least. All the way back up the canyon this tactic was employed. A squad of men would stop and engage the Indians in sporadic fire to cover the retreat whenever the Indians pressed them too close. At the top of the canyon the fleeing men began to realize they were American soldiers, the best in the world, and began to regain their composure, enabling the officers to once more assume control. A stand was made at some trees, but the Indians, with seemingly limitless reserves, threw in reinforcements, and succeeded in increasing the pressure on the already beleaguered troops. An orderly retreat was once more resumed.

By now all of the men realized their only salvation lay in an orderly withdrawal—and a strict obedience to orders. The method employed in the retreat up the canyon was once again brought into play. After this method of rear guard over running rear guard had allowed them to travel some distance, swampy ground was encountered.

This spongy turf had apparently been crossed without undue incident, but upon reaching firm soil on the far side, Lieutenant Parnell heard a desperate plea for help. Looking back he saw a man struggling on foot through the tules. The man's horse had been shot from under him and he would most certainly fall victim to the Indians unless someone did something and quick. Seeing the trooper near exhaustion from struggling in the mire, without a moment's hesitation, Lieutenant Parnell wheeled his horse and headed for the sagging man.

Racing back through the muck, Lieut. Parnell swung the man up behind him and they raced back to the main body of troops. As the fatigued troops began to near a town, a posse of civilians came to their aid.

No Indian would stand at even odds, so noting the additional firepower, they withdrew.

That evening, when roll was called, a total of 33 enlisted men and an officer, out of a complement of 90 men who had entered the canyon, did not answer their names at muster.

First Sergeant Michael McCarthy, Troop H, 1st U.S. Cavalry, "was detailed with six men to hold a commanding position and held it with great gallantry until the troops fell back. He then fought his way through the Indians, rejoined a portion of his command, and continued to fight in retreat. He had two horses shot under him, and was captured, but escaped and reported for duty after 3 days' hiding and wandering in the mountains."

First Lieutenant William R. Parnell, 1st Cavalry, "with a few men, in the face of a heavy fire from pursuing Indians and an imminent peril, returned and rescued a soldier, whose horse had been killed and who had been left behind in the retreat."

DOORWAY TO HELL

After the troops had been withdrawn from Whitebird Canyon, General O. O. Howard took to the field in pursuit of Chief Joseph and his Nez Percé, with part of the Twenty-First Infantry, First Cavalry, and Fourth Artillery, who were equipped with a mountain howitzer and two Gatling guns. Not until July 11, 1877, were the troops able to join battle with the Indians at Clearwater River, Idaho.

The conflict was as fierce as combat can get—often hand-to-hand. Unlike other Indian tribes, the Nez Percé were excellent marksmen. Many of the troopers were hit. The troops hastily constructed breastworks, behind which, the Indians accurate fire pinned them down. Several times the Indians charged. Each attack was barely beaten back by the troopers.

During one of the Indian charges, they captured the howitzer and the two Gatling guns, rolled them where they stood abandoned and useless—in no-man's land, between the lines.

All night the Indian war drums boomed. The deadly rifle fire from the Indian lines was renewed, with vigor at dawn.

Then there occurred one of those heroic incidents which proved to be the turning point of the battle. First Lieutenant Charles F. Humphrey led eleven men in a mad dash into no man's land to recapture the howitzer and Gatling guns. In the dash, three troopers were killed, two more seriously wounded, Lieut. Humphrey and another trooper were slightly wounded, but they brought back to their lines the valuable guns, their dead and wounded.

Now it was the Indians' turn to keep their heads down as howitzer shells burst among them and streams of lead sang overhead.

The infantry successfully charged the left end of the Indians' line, managed to turn it, causing the Indians to withdraw to a newer, and more formidable, position across the river. Then at their leisure, the Indians vanished into the wilderness.

Lieut. Humphrey, "voluntarily and successfully conducted, in the face of a withering fire, a party which recovered possession of an abandoned howitzer and two Gatling guns lying between the lines a few yards from the Indians."

THE LONG DAY

In the Big Hole Basin of southwestern Montana, at the foot of the eastern slope of the Continental Divide, is the Big Hole Battlefield. It was here, on a hot August day in 1877, that 200 soldiers and citizen volunteers fought desperately for their lives. Eight officers and 76 men of the 7th U.S. Infantry and 36 citizens known as the Bitteroot Volunteers, left Fort Missoula at one o'clock on the afternoon of August 4th. By marching late into the night they were able to reach Fort Owen. On August 6th, scouts excitedly reported that the fleeing Nez Percé Indians had been sighted in Ross Hole just that morning. The troops were in the saddle without so much as a cup of coffee.

Once again on the morning of August 7th, swallowing but a hasty breakfast, the troops pushed through Ross Hole to the foot of the main Divide. That night a small force of civilian and army volunteers made a march in an effort to cut off the Indians by capturing their pony herd, which was hoped would cripple their flight to the extent of holding them until the soldiers could catch up. As the main body of men reached the summit of the Divide, at an elevation of 6,995 feet, word was received that the advance detail had located the Nez Percé camp, but the terrain in the Divide was so rugged it would take several hours before the pony herd could be reached and a surprise attack was, therefore, out of the question. The troops ate yet another cold meal and washed it down with water.

127

At 11:00 o'clock that night, August 8, the troops were aroused from a lethargic sleep and quickly and quietly formed into a line of march. Each man was issued 90 rounds of extra ammunition and a day's ration of food. Then, on a black and moonless night, they stumbled and struggled along through the morbid gloom of the forest, past huge rocks and fallen timber, through bone-chilling creeks and sucking mud, until more open ground was encountered on the bluffs above Ruby Creek. There before them lay the Big Hole and the Indian camp they had endured such hardships to find.

As the men sat their mounts in the pre-dawn gloom, eyes fixed on the Indian village, it seemed almost impossible the Indians did not know of their presence. As the eastern sky began to brighten into a dull glow, the Indian camp nestled in the willows along the Big Hole began to stir for the business of the dawning day. In the growing light, the soldiers were sent into the bottomland with orders to advance through the willow thickets as quietly as was possible. As the left end of the blue clad line was pushing its way through the thick brush, a young mounted Indian suddenly appeared. Before he could recover from his surprise, the Indian youth was shot dead through the heart. Knowing full well that the sound of this shot would alarm the Indian camp, the soldiers plunged forward through the water and unloosed a volley of carbine fire into the Indians who were by this time rushing from their teepees.

As the sun lunged from behind the mountains that August 9th, a desperate and deadly struggle began to take form. Within 20 minutes of the shot which killed the Indian youth, the troops were in possession of the Indian camp and they quickly began to carry out the orders for its complete destruction.

Recovering from the initial and surprise panic, the Nez Percé began to rally. So savagely did they turn upon the troops with their accurate rifle fire, the troopers were forced to forget the destruction of the camp and go on defense, to remain alive.

Even though the troops had fired part of the village, it did not burn and their position soon became extremely untenable. The Indian fire forced them to retire to a little timbered bench above the river at the foot of the mountain. Then they began a savage struggle for their lives.

By the time the soldiers had attained their new position, their situation to all intents and purposes was improved only slightly, if at all.

The Indians began to climb into the tall pine trees growing profusely everywhere, and began pouring a telling fire into the blue ranks.

In a frenzied haste men scraped out shallow rifle pits. Trees were felled and used as a scanty cover in conjunction with the shallow holes. Wherever the lay of the land offered some sort of protection it was put to good use. Concealed as they were, some merely by foliage of the felled trees, the troopers returned the Indians' fire throughout the long, weary hours of that long, hot August day.

Late in the day, the Indians fired the tall grass and, as the flames swept forward, the troops were ordered to be on the alert for an Indian attack under cover of the smoke and flames. Should an attack occur, the troops were ordered to charge through the flames and deliver a smart counter attack. Fortunately for the soldiers, the wind changed and blew the flames back onto the Indians, where they petered into a few wisps of harmless smoke.

All day long the August sun blazed relentlessly and acrid fumes from burnt powder, mixed with the clinging smoke from the grass fire, cut the throats and nostrils of the wounded men in almost unbearable pain, yet not one man uttered a word of complaint. The men fit to man the rifle pits on the firing line sucked pebbles in their mouths in an attempt to excite the glands. All that day their only food was meat cut from a dead horse and eaten raw. With dead and wounded on every side, the gallant little band seemed to be doomed to its fate—but they never once showed any sign of weakening. They fought hard and they died hard.

The wagons, with ammunition, food and medicine, had been left behind, also a mountain howitzer. The following morning as the pack train came forward, six men left the wagons with the howitzer, with the intention of relieving the pressure on the beleaguered troops. Many times the howitzer did little or no apparent damage as the slow moving round could be heard as it approached, giving the Indians more than sufficient time to seek cover. But it was the eerie sound of the ball and the necessity to lower the head that made the howitzer effective, although during the Indian campaigns the artillery claimed its share of casualties.

The howitzer was emplaced on a hill overlooking the battlefield. Because the gun held such a strategic position, the Indians mounted an attack up the hill and managed to overrun the gun, after it had fired but twice. Two of the six-man gun crew panicked and bolted to safety, and as the Indians threw the gun from its trunnion, the four remaining soldiers fought with rifle, pistol, knife and hand. But the odds were just too great.

Corporal Robert E. Sale was killed outright. Sergeants Frederics and Daly were gravely wounded. Private Bennett, driver of the horses hauling the howitzer, was pinned under one of the wounded animals and by feigning death, escaped after the Indians withdrew.

All through the night of August 9th, with one third of the entire command listed as casualties, the situation was as desperate at the Big Hole as it had been at Beecher's Island when survival seemed ever so remote.

Sgt. William D. Edwards volunteered to make an attempt to go for help. Cautiously he crawled through the Indian lines on his belly, and then walked more than forty miles to a mining camp known as French Gulch, where he borrowed a horse and rode forty miles more to Deer Lodge, Montana. Not once did he stop to rest.

Sergeant Wilson volunteered to attempt to seek outside help when it was feared Edwards might have been killed. Sergeant Wilson, too, succeeded in reaching Deer Lodge. Both are epic journeys almost equal to that of "Portagee Phillips," but which have been lost to history in the accounts of the Battle of the Big Hole.

As soon as dawn appeared, the Nez Percé resumed their deadly sniping pouring a steady fire into the troopers' slowly diminishing ranks. Some of those less severely wounded refused to leave the firing line until wounded again and yet then again and were, by then, compelled to call it quits. That evening, as relief drew near, the Indians, with a derisive parting volley, withdrew.

At Big Hole, Montana, 9 August 1877, Private Lorenzo Brown, 7th Infantry, "after having been severely wounded in right shoulder, continued to do duty in a most courageous manner." Private Wilfred Clard. 2nd Cavalry, showed "conspicuous gallantry, especial skill as a sharpshooter." First Sergeant William D. Edwards, 7th Infantry, "bravery in action." Musician John McLennon, 7th Infantry, "gallantry in action." Sergeant Patrick Rogan, 7th Infantry, "verified and reported the company while subjected to a galling fire from the enemy." Sergeant Mildren H. Wilson, 7th Infantry, "gallantry in forming company from line of skirmishers and deploying again under a galling fire and in carrying dispatches at the imminent risk of his life.

THE SCHOOL OF SOLDIERY

By now a winter had passed and also a summer, when Sergeant Henry Hogan's star shone brightly once more. The Nez Percé (Pierced Nose) Indians, under their leader, Chief Joseph, were a fiercely independent tribe of Indians. When gold was discovered in Montana and Idaho, a route called the Bozeman Trail was opened between Fort Laramie, Wyoming, and the wilderness. It bisected some of the best Indian grounds that were to be found anywhere. To make the trail safe for settlers and gold seekers, a string of military posts was built approximately one-hundred miles apart along the Bozeman Trail. Some of these posts bore the names of such illustrious American fighting men as Phil Kearney, Reno, and C. F. Smith and it was near these forts that many of the bloodiest battles of the Indian wars were fought.

Despite the dangers, the hardships, the elements, and the land, the homesteaders and gold miners kept coming in increasing numbers.

In time, all of the Indian tribes along the Bozeman Trail were subdued, but one—the Nez Percé. They refused to budge an inch. In 1876, the Nez Percé went on the warpath. The tactics of their leader, Chief Joseph, are now legend. At a grand council in 1877, Joseph decided to move his tribe to the north into Canada where the white soldiers would have to leave the Nez Percé in peace. Thus began the now famous long march of the Nez Percé through Idaho and Montana. Slowed down by

133

women and children, Joseph avoided any pitched battles with the persistent pony soldiers that he was able to.

When Joseph and his people were but a short forty miles from the Canadian border, a column was ordered to cut him off from his goal.

On the morning of 30 September 1877, in the shadow of Bear's Paw Mountain (like the Little Big Horn, now Little Bighorn, the Bear's Paw has been Bear Paws, and is now Bearpaw), scouts reported the Indians had set up their camp in a kidney-shaped ravine, circled by heavily wooded bluffs. The number of teepees indicated the army had discovered the entire Nez Percé tribe in the ravine.

This looked like it would be easy and quick. In 30 degree weather, a detachment of cavalry went thundering down upon the camp. However, this group of the Army had not had much experience with Joseph. One did not charge him blindly. It suddenly became obvious to the charging troopers that noe a single Indian was to be seen anywhere. Sometime during the early morning hours, the entire Nez Percé tribe had left, leaving fire burning to deceive those who followed.

Then, without warning, a hail of rifle bullets hit the blue line. Elements of the 2nd Cavalry were ordered to capture the Indian pony herd while behind every tree, every bush and every boulder, on the bluffs surrounding the ravine. Indians were methodically picking off the troopers with deadly accuracy.

In almost less time than it takes to relate the events, almost half of the troopers and all of the officers were either wounded or dead. Joseph had instructed his sharpshooting braves to pick off the officers first. A second wave was sent charging directly into the storm of lead being poured into them from the heights.

While the 2nd was busily engaged with the pony herd, the 7th Cavalry charged a ridge where they faced a deadly blast of rifle fire from above. Army saddles were emptied all along the 7th's line. The men of the 7th dismounted, deployed and surged ahead. Close to the summit of its objective, the 7th was forced to halt, but it was able to hold the ground it had attained. The 7th suffered 53 per cent casualties in its charge.

Joseph still held parts of his camp and the heights above, all the while strengthening his position by constructing breastworks.

A second wave of cavalry was sent in to support the 7th, but the slope proved to be too steep for the horses to negotiate, so the troopers were forced to abandon their mounts about midway up the sides of the slope, leaving the men perfect targets for the Indian marksmen.

Behind this second wave of cavalry came the infantry, which included Company G and Sergeant Hogan. Dropping down behind a dead horse, Hogan waited until he saw the yellow flash of an Indian rifle and then he aimed his shot a few inches below the flash.

Troopers littered the sloope everywhere Hogan looked and they continued to fall in alarming numbers. It was settled down to two simple choices. Storm the bluffs and dislodge the Indians, or retreat. The word "retreat" has always been a nasty word in the mouth of American fighting men, so it boiled down to a dislodgement of the Indians.

Sergeant Hogan started up the slope on his hands and knees, using brush and boulder for whatever cover they would provide.

Suddenly the man on Hogan's right threw up his arms, uttered a cry of anguish and fell over backwards. Sergeant Hogan at once recognized Lieutenant Romeyn of A Company. A dark red spot was spreading rapidly on the lower portion of the officer's tunic. Without hesitation, Sergeant Hogan quickly grabbed the lieutenant under arms and crawled back down the slope, slipping and sliding, tenderly as possible, dragging the lieutenant's body with him.

At the bottom of the slope, Sergeant Hogan paused only long enough to catch his breath, then, once more picking up the wounded officer, this time in a fireman's carry, staggered across the clearing to his lines, exposed the entire distance to the deadly fire of the Indians on the bluff. Eager hands relieved Hogan of his burden. Without hesitation, Sergeant

Hogan returned at once to the slope and started inching his way up the steep sides of the bluff. He quickly caught up with the rest of the troopers storming the slopes, who had, by now, worked their way to within 50 yards of the top.

It seemed impossible that the Indian fire could increase in intensity, but as Sergeant Hogan inched his way up the steep sides of the slope, the Indian fire increased in volume. Foot by foot, yard by yard, the men moved ever forward over the frozen ground.

At point-blank range the Indians couldn't miss. Men fell all around the Sergeant. Then they were among the Indians, fighting hand-to-hand, with knife, rock and fist. Unable to withstand such determination, the Indians broke and retreated to the woods.

Completely exhausted, and almost out of ammunition, the troops made no attempt at pursuit. As long as the troops held the Indian village, the Indians were doomed to the elements. The soldiers regrouped and formed a defensive position in anticipation of an Indian counterattack which never materialized. For four more days the Indians held out, then Joseph came forth to deliver his message in which he stated he would fight no more. The war with the Nez Percé was over.

The troopers counted their casualties—twenty-four dead, forty-two wounded. Lieutenant Romeyn recovered from his wound. Sergeant Hogan received his second Medal of Honor.

Other Medals were awarded to First Lieutenant George W. Baird; First Lieutenant Mason Carter; Captain Edward S. Godfrey; Second Lieutenant Oscar F. Long; Second Lieutenant Edward J. McClernard; Captain Myles Moylan; First Lieutenant Henry Romeyn; Major and Surgeon Henry R. Tilton, U. S. Army.

RELENTLESS, DOGGED PURSUIT

On 17th July 1881, eighty-year-old Nana, war chief of the Apaches, ambushed a pack train of the 9th U.S. Cavalry in the Cuchillo Negro Mountains, New Mexico. This was the first indication as to the whereabouts of the wily old Nana.

The Negro troops quickly swung in pursuit of the maurauding Indians. The trail led the troopers through Canyon del Perro to a small ranch near Arena Blanca. Overeager scouts gave the troopers away and the Indians once more took to flight.

Toward the San Andreas Mountains, the Indians fled. Once again the black troops pursued, took up positions and charged. Nothing! Once more the Indians had fled, leaving a trail of mockery. News of the wandering band was next to nil until July 30, when the horribly mutilated bodies of four Mexicans were discovered in the San Mateo Mountains.

A rancher recruited a group of thirty-six civilians and set out in pursuit of the elusive old Nana.

On August 1, the civilians had ridden up a canyon and then stopped for the noon meal. Horses had been unsaddled and turned loose to graze. A lackluster guard lounged sleepily near the herd while the rest of the party sat down to eat. With a series of wild yells and a drum-roll-like rifle volley, the Indians easily ran off the civilians' horses. The civilians opened a weak fire and the Indians quickly dropped eight of them.

Had old Nana chosen to, at this time, he could have wiped out the whole civilian band, but he had gotten what he wanted most—the horses.

Two days later, the black troops were on old Nana's trail again. Doggedly they followed the Indians' trail which led through the Red Canyon, and more dead Mexicans. The command was relentlessly driven to the limit and finally caught up with the Indians again near the Santa Monica Springs, but with a couple of derisive volleys, the Indians vanished as they had before.

For nine long days, through the desert La Savoya to Carrizo Canyon, the troops followed in relentless, dogged pursuit. They did not allow the Indians any time to rest. Pursuit. Relentless, dogged pursuit. That was the watchword. On 12 August, the troopers ran head on into the Apaches. Though completely outnumbered, the small band of nineteen troopers went into action. A short fire fight ensued and once again the Indians melted into the underbrush. The troopers had suffered one dead and three wounded. Plans were made to take care of the dead and wounded and the pursuit was taken again as soon as feasible.

Sergeant Thomas Shaw, 8th U. S. Cavalry, "forced the enemy back after stubbornly holding his ground in an extremely exposed position and prevented the enemy's superior numbers from surrounding his command."

Cuchillo Negro means Black Knife, after a Mimbreno Apache Chieftain, and is a mountain in New Mexico. In August 1881, southern Mexico swarmed with soldiers. On 16 August, in the Shadow of Cuchillo Negro, old Nana, who had succeeded Victorio, the great Mimbreno chief, just four days since he had had his fight with Captain Parker and the 8th Cavalry at Carrizo Canyon, turned viciously upon his pursuers to test the mettle of the black troopers once again.

From a good concealing cover, with never a sign as to where they were lurking, the Indians sneaked through the mesquite and cactus.

Courageously the black troops fought back, giving an excellent account of themselves, but they were unable to cope with such a savage enemy.

Second Lieutenant George R. Burnett, second-in-command, 9th U. S. Cavalry, "saved the life of a dismounted soldier, who was in imminent danger of being cut off, by alone galloping quickly to his assistance under heavy fire and escorting him to a place of safety, his horse being shot twice in the action."

Two troopers had been killed in the short action. A good share of the troopers' horses had been killed or crippled by the Apaches' fire.

Once the Apaches figured they had crippled the troopers to the extent where they knew the troopers would be unable to follow, they quickly and easily beat off another attack by the troopers and withdrew.

Private Agustus Walley, "bravery in action with hostile Indians."

First Sergeant Moses Williams, "rallied a detachment, skillfully conducted a running fight of 3 or 4 hours, and by his coolness, bravery, and unflinching devotion to duty in standing by his commanding officer in an exposed position under a heavy fire from a large party of Indians saved the lives of at least three of his comrades."

Nana next headed south, but before he left the United States, he stopped to teach the soldiers one more lesson.

This time it was another detachment of twenty troopers from the 9th Cavalry who went toiling in pursuit of old Nana's trail south. Near McEver's ranch, New Mexico, on 18 August 1881, old Nana and his tired and outnumbered band once more chose their ground wisely. The staccato rattle of their first volleys was the first hint the pursuers had that they had caught up with their foe.

The Apaches' fire was wicked and deadly. Here and there a trooper dropped, leaving a hole in the line, a victim of the Apaches' deadly fire. The officer in command of the troops fell dead. This ended the fight. Six troopers were dead, including the officer.

Old Nana had made his point. The Indians drew off to the border, crossing it at their leisure unimpeded.

Sergeant Brent Woods, 9th Cavalry, "saved the lives of his comrades and citizens of the detachment."

ONLY THE BRAVE

No opposing forces in the history of the world ever differed more radically than did the Army of the United States and the hostile Indians of the American West. In the battles with the American Indian, the trooper was engaged in an occupation which was not apt to add much to his fame or personal comfort. To him it was all danger and extreme hardships, but of such ingredients are brave men composed.

In the early 1880's, Fort Apache, Arizona, was garrisoned by two troops of the 6th Cavalry; two companies of the 12th Infantry; and a detachment of Indian scouts.

Among the junior officers stationed at the post were First Lieutenant William H. Carter and Second Lieutenant Thomas Cruse, both assigned to the 6th Cavalry. Lieut. Carter was to be cited for "the rescue of, with the voluntary assistance of two soldiers, the wounded under a heavy fire." Tommy Cruse would have to wait until the following year at the battle of Big Dry Fork to win his Medal of Honor. Also assigned to the 6th Cavalry were Sergeant Alonzo Bowman and Private Richard Heartery.

An Indian had begun a dance he claimed would return people from the dead. People who wanted to believe him did. The idea and dance raced through the Indians like a prairie fire. They began to dance. They danced for 45 days and nights. The longer they danced, the more intoxicated with the idea they became. It wasn't too long before some of the excitement spread to a small group of Indian scouts at the fort.

Around 4:00 P.M. on Sunday, 28 August 1881, orders were received to "capture if possible or kill" the originator of the dance. About 8:00 A.M. the following day, 85 officers and men, accompanied by 23 Indian scouts, filed out the gates of the fort and headed northwest toward the Cibicu. After covering about one-half of their scheduled march they went into bivouac for the night.

The march was resumed early Tuesday morning 30 August 1881, and by 2:00 P.M. they had reached the valley of the Cibicu.

Swarms of painted savages buzzed around the command as it neared the dreamer's tabernacle of branches and twigs covered with blankets and rags. One Indian warrior of exceedingly evil visage, galloped up to Lieut. Cruse brandishing a rifle and a pistol.

As the troopers wheeled into line facing the filthy wickiup, they espied their quarry lying on a heap of dirty blankets.

An officer and an interpreter moved forward, informing the dreamer (named Bobby) that the dances must cease immediately and he (Bobby) accompany the troops back to the fort. Bobby listened intently to the interpreter while his sullen devotees, their dark shoulders powdered with a sacred yellow pollen, clustered about in a very threatening manner. Bobby volunteered to give himself up in three or four days, an offer which was refused. Bobby was once again told to prepare himself to return to the fort—and NOW!

The troops would brook no more delay and no more nonsense. As the order was translated, everyone could sense the charged tension in the air. This was going to be war.

One of the Indian scouts performed a brave action which forestalled any immediate shooting. The scout entered the teepee, picked up Bobby, who offered no resistance, carried him outside and boosted him up on a horse. The column filed out of the camp which was threatening to explode into violence at any moment and headed in the direction of the fort.

Before the entire column could clear the Indian camp, the

142

Indians threatened to upset the troops orderly manner but even though it was close, the troops got away with their prisoner.

After the column had put more than two miles between them and the Indian camp, they halted on a small meadow which was about ten feet above the bed of the Cibicu. Horses and pack mules were unsaddled.

The dreamer was placed, under heavy guard, in a square formed by the pack equipment.

Meanwhile, the Indians had followed the troopers and amid the confusion of the troops unpacking, the Indians sneaked across the Cibicu and converged on the campsite.

Lieut. Carter was ordered to clear the troublesome Indians from the meadow where the troops were bivouacked.

When Lieut. Carter ordered the Indians to move on, they halted and began to mill about uncertainly. Some half-witted young buck emitted a hideous war-cry, raised his repeating Winchester over his head and fired, precipitating the long-expected explosion. A hundred other guns boomed. Bullets thudded into camp equipment and soldiers alike, snapping and buzzing overhead. Troopers scrambled for cover and prepared to return the Indians' fire. Both sides blazed away with rifle and pistol. Bullets flew about even as men engaged in hand-to-hand combat.

An officer on either side of Lieut. Carter was killed instantly, but by some unseen providence Lieut. Carter remained unscathed. Some of the loyal scouts became excited and began to fire at the soldiers.

An order was given to kill Bobby. One of the troopers shot him, but succeeded only in wounding him in the thigh, then the trooper collapsed, shot by the scouts. Bobby endeavored to reach the scouts, exhorting them to fight the soldiers, yelling that if he were killed, he would come to life again. A mere boy of a trumpeter jammed his pistol down Bobby's throat and pulled the trigger, inflicting a stunning, though unbelievably non-fatal wound.

Suddenly, Bobby's pony appeared from out of the seeming nowhere, his 16-year-old son aboard, charging wildly through the camp searching for his father. He was killed for his loyal though brash bravery.

Lieut. Carter cleared the Indians from his side of the camp and in sizing up the situation he noticed an officer's body lying about 100 yards beyond the line of soldiers. At great peril to himself and the two men, Lieut. Carter, along with Privates Bird and Berry, rushed to the fallen officer and retrieved his dead body.

The Indians now loosed a terrific fire upon this party, mortally wounding Bird and inflicting a grievous wound to Berry's shoulder.

As soon as Lieut. Carter had turned the dead officer's body over to other soldiers, he once more braved the wall of Indian rifle fire to bring in the dead body of Private Bird. According to those who witnessed this deed, they testified it had been accomplished under the heaviest fire any of them had ever witnessed. Trooper Berry died of his wound within the hour.

While all of this had been taking place, no one had paid much attention to Bobby, who it was ssumed, was dead. He was discovered crawling about on his hands and knees delirious, but tenacious to the thread of life. A sergeant standing close by picked up a camp axe and buried it in the dreamer's skull. This time he was dead and no one present believed he would come to life again.

As darkness descended, as was their custom, the Indians withdrew.

The troopers quickly gathered up their dead comrades, dug a common grave and tenderly placed the bodies of the one officer and six troopers into it, making no attempt whatsoever to bury Bobby. As the last sad strains of taps floated over the valley of the Cibicu, the column, now mostly dismounted through the loss of mounts, filed silently away toward Fort Apache.

The closest guard was maintained throughout the night. Lieut. Cruse, with the remainder of the loyal scouts, rode point. Several times the column was forced to halt and then

144

had to proceed with the utmost caution past Indian camps, where the savages waited, fully expecting to annihilate the troopers come first light of the next day. Lieut. Cruse inadvertently took a wrong fork in the trail and when realization came of this mistake, he made great haste to catch up with the main body. Upon his arrival he now became the rear guard instead of the point. Another of the badly wounded troopers passed on during the night and his body was lashed to a horse so the column could continue its perilous journey. The troops reached the fort, and safety with no further incidents.

DOT DASH DOT

A small garrison of troopers was deployed over the San Carlos Reservation and Fort Apache, Arizona. They were connected to the Agency and Fort Thomas, via the telegraph. Private William C. Barnes had come to Fort Apache in the 1880's as a Morse code operator.

Some Chiricahua renegades crossed the border from Mexico and committed crimes against the whites in Arizona. They infiltrated the reservation, creating trouble and disrupting the wire service by repeatedly cutting the wires.

Each time the wires were cut, Barnes and Private Pike had to search out the break and repair it. Over and over again this pair conducted this tedious—and always dangerous—work. On 10 September 1881, the line went dead at a most inopportune time. The break had to be located quickly, so out Barnes and Pike went.

They returned shortly with a wounded Indian who told a story of a detachment of troopers who were all dead and that Fort Apache was next.

Private Barnes thought he could take up a commanding position on a butte overlooking the fort and from there warn the fort of any Indians' approach. Burdened with a canteen, binoculars, signal flares and weapons, he topped the butte. Along toward mid-afternoon, his binoculars picked up the first traces of dust of approaching horsemen from the direction of the Cibicu. He continued to track them with the binoculars until a shot from the fort recaptured his attention. Pike signaled him—Indians below—come down. Barnes could see that by now he had been cut off so he signaled Pike to look for him after dark.

The sun was pretty well down by the time Barnes could be certain the dust cloud was created by returning troops. His elation at seeing the troopers caused Barnes' reasoning to take the form of bravado. Swinging into his saddle, he charged down the trail. As he neared the Indians, who were secreted in a sheltered thicket, he spurred his flagging mount into a breakneck gallop, firing his pistol right and left into the thick brush as he went thundering past.

The Indians, now caught completely off guard, offered little response.

An hour later, the advance guard of the oncoming column, with carbines at the ready, challenged him.

Barnes reined in his mount and identified himself. It was then he learned that he had ridden *into* a circling ring of Indians. The only help which could be counted on was at Fort Thomas, 90 miles away on the Gila River. Because he had a smattering of knowledge of the surrounding country, Barnes volunteered to go for help. He was placed aboard a sturdy, fleet and sure-footed cavalry mount. He shed all cumbersome equipment save pistol and canteen.

Knowing all routes were sure to be patrolled by hostiles, Barnes angled away from the well traveled routes toward a little-known trail that led to High Mesa. The path, easily followed by day, had to be sought out by night. Allowing his horse to pick its own way he headed for Black River Crossing. But the Apaches held sway over the crossing. The river was high. He could not turn back. He decided to swim the swollen torrent. Cutting his saddle blanket into strips he wrapped them around the hooves of his mount. He worked his way to the river's edge. The roar of the surging water kept his presence from being detected by the mongrel dogs of the Indian villages. He passed within less than one hundred yards of the Indians.

Hanging his pistol belt around his neck, he urged his horse into the raging, muddy water. Almost at once, the horse began to swim vigorously and in a short time stood on the opposite bank. Then the horse expelled air loudly and the Indian camp was instantly astir. Several Indians started to shoot in Barnes's direction. His horse had lost the blanket strips covering his hooves and every step on the rock bordering the river produced a metallic clang, making Barnes a moving target. He was showered with foliage as bullets bit off branches and bits of bark and bullets ricocheted off the rock.

About mid-morning the next day, Barnes met two troopers out of Fort Thomas who took his dispatches back to the fort with them. They told Barnes the whole countryside was astir. Private Barnes rode back to Fort Apache and sighted nary a single Indian on his way. He was called to the parade grounds where the whole garrison was drawn up in formation.

All of the officers, including General George Crook wore gold braided uniforms. The General read the citation: "bravery in action", saluted and shook Pvt. Barnes's hand.

THAT FIGHTING FOURTH

On April 20th, 1882, every telegraph key in every military post on the Mexican border was clicking furiously. The Chiricahua Apaches, led by Loco, had struck on the American side of the border. Within an hour of the raid at San Carlos, troops all along the border had answered "Boots and Saddles" and were ready to move. By dawn of the next day, they were hot on the trail of Loco. On the morning of 23 April, a small trail, less than twelve hours old, was struck in the Stein's Peak Range which led the troops toward the Gila River.

Two prongs of the fourth Cavalry were busily probing for fresh Indian sign. It was terribly hot and the dust was so thick, it was almost impossible to breath. Suddenly the main column espied a lone rider lashing his horse across the desert, his desperate haste bringing him in their direction. As the rider approached, he proved to be a dispatch rider. He panted out the story that one of the satellite detachments, searching for fresh Indian sign, had been ambushed in Horseshoe Canyon. Several troopers were dead and the rest fighting for their lives.

The main column almost rode their horses to the ground as they hurried across the hot plain. As they neared the mountains, the clatter of carbine and pistol fire could easily be heard. The main column experienced little difficulty in penetrating the Indians' line to exact a timely rescue of the scouting party. They they heard this story.

The Indians had ambushed the scouting detachment. So sure were the Indians of the fate of the trapped men, they delayed their attack long enough for the main column to appear.

Now the Indians found themselves on defense. Now it was the Army's turn to be reluctant to attack the Indians who had taken up extremely strong defensive positions. However, the fighting 4th sent two columns to right and left in flanking maneuvers while the third column remained in the center. Under a heavy fire, they steadily advanced. Suffering heavy casualties, the Indians slowly withdrew.

Wagoner John Schnitzer and First Lieutenant Wilber E. Wilder were awarded Medals for "assisting under a heavy fire, to rescue a wounded comrade."

THIS IS A HELL OF A GOOD PLACE TO DIE

Although this was no Chiricahua Mountains campaign where 31 Medals of Honor had been awarded, the Army has always been proud of the battle of Big Dry Wash, Arizona, as a fitting finale to its role in fighting one of the two most troublesome tribes of Indians on the North American continent, the Apaches of Arizona. There remained plenty of activity, of course.

Genorimo had not yet been heard from, but the fighting that developed later was mostly between hostiles and Indian scouts. After Big Dry Wash, the major fighting between the troopers and the Apaches had passed into history.

Second Lieutenant Thomas Cruse, 6th Cavalry, "gallantly charged hostile Indians and with his carbine compelled a party of them to keep under cover of their breastworks, thus being enabled to recover a severely wounded soldier."

Second Lieutenant George H. Morgan, 3rd Cavalry, "gallantly held his ground at a critical moment and fired upon the advancing enemy (hostile Indians) until himself disabled by a shot."

First Sergeant Charles Taylor, 3rd Cavalry, "gallantry in action."

First Sergeant Frank West, 6th Cavalry, "rallied his command and led it in the advance against the enemy's fortified position."

On the 4th of July, 1882, the soldiers gathered in Tucson,

Arizona, to celebrate Independence Day. Apache renegades also gathered in Tucson to organize their own sort of celebration. Two days after the 4th, the chief of Indian police was shot from ambush by some of the same Apache renegades. They made one big mistake, however. The dastardly deed was witnessed by a friendly Indian who quickly spread the alarm to whites on their way home from Tucson to Globe. As soon as they got the word the Army swung into action.

Even though the telegraph was comparatively new, several troops of soldiers were in the field within hours. Several forced marches carried prongs of converging columns to a supposed common center, where the renegades were suspected to be. Two troops of the 3rd Cavalry out of Fort Thomas, Arizona, cut the renegades' trail and pressed them so rapidly, they were unable to indulge in widespread destruction. Still they managed to slay nearly a dozen whites as they hurried north. Four troops of the 3rd and four troops of the 6th Cavalry were hurriedly ordered to take the field from Fort Apache, Arizona, and attempt to intercept the renegades at the Salt River Crossing.

One troop from each regiment was hastened eastward from Camp Verde, Arizona, to prevent the renegades from reaching the sanctuary of the Navajo Reservation to the north. Two troops from the 3rd and two troops from the 6th were dispatched from Fort Whipple, Arizona, with instructions to head for the Tonto Basin. Still other troops were dispatched from Fort McDowell, Arizona. The troops from Fort Whipple cut diagonally southeastward across incredibly rough country until they too had cut the renegades' trail. The columns from Fort Apache had marched swiftly from the Cibicu to the Salt Crossing, about where Roosevelt Dam stands today. Finding the track of the renegades turning north, they joined in the hot pursuit. As was military protocol, the command of the coming battle would fall to the first officer to locate the renegades, regardless of rank.

Not too far to the north was the great cliff of the Mogollon Rim. The renegades, no doubt, would seek to ambush the commands at the point where the tortuous path snaked its way down into the gash known as Big Dry Wash, also Chevelon's Fork of the Canyon Diablo, or the Big Dry Wash.

About 3:00 P.M. on 17 July 1882, scouts crept out onto the rim of Big Dry Wash Canyon. It seems incredible, but the Indian scallywags were discerned by sharp-eyed scouts on the opposite cliff, about 700 yards distant. The problem was now how to get to them.

The command of battle fell to Captain Adna Chaffee. He deployed the men along the rim of the chasm, the renegades apparently oblivious to their movements. Captain Chaffee sent parties to the right and to the left to force a crossing of the canyon above and below the trail, and then get in a position to the rear of the renegades who seemed busily engaged in setting up their own ambush.

Unfortunately, a nervous recruit couldn't resist temptation and, raising his carbine, fired before Chaffee was ready. The renegades quickly returned fire with vigor. An officer fell first, when a renegade .44 slug hit a rock, split into fragments, and one of the fragments penetrated the officer's eye.

Lieut. Cruse had been ordered to cross the canyon below the trail. Working his way well over a mile to the southeast of the fighting, he found a way down the precipitous cliff all the way to the bottom of the gorge. So steep and narrow was the canyon at this point that from its bottom, stars could be seen shining brightly overhead in the afternoon sky framed between its steep vertical sides.

Lieut. Morgan had been sent to the left to cross the canyon above the trail. As he was making his way, the Indians, attempting a flanking maneuver of their own, fell upon him. A torrent of gunfire erupted between them. At about the same time this phase of the action was taking place, Lieut. Cruse discovered the Indian pony herd well down in the canyon. Appropriating the pony herd, the rest of the command grunted their way up out of the canyon, raced across the intervening ground and fell upon the renegades' rear. The Indians, unable to withstand well directed volley fire, panicked and milled

155

their way backward to where they had left the pony herd. All the while the troopers continued to pour a heavy fire into the ranks of the renegades. By now, it was late in the afternoon and the shadows began to lengthen quickly.

Lieut. Morgan raised himself up from behind some fallen logs to get a better shot, but was instead shot through the arm, the bullet passing into his body.

Lieut. Cruse, on the canyon rim about 200 yards in front of what had been the renegades' original position, fearing the renegades might escape, wanted to mount a charge against the enemy's position. He was informed that many of the Indians were still alive and full of fight, yet he leaped to his feet and charged directly at the Indians. He soon found out his buddies had been right about many of the Indians still being alive and they all seemed to be shooting at him. A renegade suddenly appeared little more than an arm's length away from Leiut. Cruse, raised his rifle and fired. The bullet missed Lieut. Cruse, but struck a trooper directly to his rear. Lieut. Cruse shot the Indian dead with his pistol and then dove for cover.

Lieut. Cruse's impromptu charge had the effect of forcing the renegades from their places of concealment. Many were shot dead and the rest put to flight. Lieut. Cruse's charge had broken the back of the Indian resistance and changed the tide of battle. As the troopers pushed forward, Lieut. Cruse, still under heavy fire, dragged the wounded trooper struck by the Indian bullet he had pistoled, back to safety, covered him with a blanket and made him as comfortable as possible. He was dead in two hours.

Darkness made it too late to pursue matters further. A rainstorm accompanied by thunder, lightning and hail caused a suspension of all operations. Under cover of the storm, the renegades still alive slunk away, their trail being washed away by the storm.

THOSE RAGGED, RUGGED TROOPERS

"Orders: Capture Geronimo. Commanding officers are expected to continue a pursuit until captured, or until they are assured a fresh command is on the trail."

Every waterhole in Arizona, no matter how small, was guarded. Every ranch had a garrison. The International Boundary between the United States and Mexico did not exist in a common cause.

Chasing the Apache was something the Army had been unable to do successfully for many, many years. A band of Membreno, White Mountain and Chiricahua Apache scouts was formed and on 11 November 1885, they left Fort Bowie, New Mexico, and a few days later, crossed the border into Mexico. Deep into the Sierra Madre Mountains they probed.

Moving mostly by night, suffering extreme hardships, the command moved ever toward the Espinosa del Diablo, the Devil's Backbone. On 9 January 1886, the scouts located an Apache *rancheria*. All that night the troopers toiled over hazardous, tiny mountain trails, crossing and recrossing a turbulent river several times as it led them down into a gorge in which the Apache *rancheria* was supposed to be. Just as the first gray streaks of dawn were stabbing the sky, as the men began to look to their weapons, a bunch of captured burros in the Indian camp began to bray loudly and long.

The Indians were saved from surprise.

Neither side suffered any casualties in the brief, but violent fire-fight that followed. The Indians abandoned their supplies which were quickly piled and destroyed, a lesson well learned by the troopers.

On 11 January, a detachment of Mexican irregulars encountered the troops' outpost, hunting the same quarry as they were.

The Mexicans, mistaking the Army Apache scouts as part of their prey, opened an erratic fire. As the officer commanding the U.S. troops rushed forward in an attempt to halt the errant fire, he fell forward on his face, mortally wounded. In an instant, the whole of the blue line blazed with fire. First Lieutenant Marion P. Maus rushed forward and dragged the wounded officer back to the troopers' line. He was still alive, but death was imminent. Lieut. Maus had a littler fashioned and the wounded officer placed upon it in preparation for returning to Fort Bowie.

The Mexicans, outnumbering the Americans two to one, insolently demanded food. Lieut. Maus moved forward in an attempt to pacify their demands and was seized and held prisoner. Explaining the situation to the irregulars, Lieut. Maus was at last released.

Marion P. Maus, First Lieutenant, First U.S. Cavalry, at Sierra Madre Mountains, Mexico, 11 January 1886, "most distinguished gallantry in action with hostile Apaches led by Geronimo and Natchez."

When the Medal of Honor was pinned on him, the White Mountain and Chiricahua Apaches beat the ground with their feathered prayer sticks and sang guttural songs. The star of the Great White Father was strong medicine. Stronger even than the hands of Geronimo.

By now Geronimo had gotten the jump on the soldiers. Up the Santa Cruz Valley he raided. Troops immediately took up the chase. On 5 May 1886. Geronimo halted in the Pinito Mountains, in northern Sonora, thirty miles south of the border. As soon as the men of the Tenth Cavalry could overtake him, they launched a vigorous attack. Because the Indians were well entrenched in the heights above them, the troopers

158

were unable to dislodge them from their positions. The troops fell back in order.

Left out in the open, where Indian bullets combed the ground everywhere, lay the prostrate form of a wounded trooper, so badly wounded he was unable to drag himself to cover. The troopers kept up a heavy and continuing volume of fire upon the Indian lines, attempting to protect their fallen comrade, but it was quite evident the wounded man could not escape sure death for long, unable to help himself.

Lying behind some sheltering rocks, Second Lieutenant Powhaten H. Clarke, fresh out of West Point, could stand it no longer. Without saying a word to anyone, he leaped to his feet and made a dash to the wounded man. A hail of lead from the Apache lines churned up the turf around his feet, but Lieut. Clarke reached the wounded man, lifted him, turned and staggered back to safety. During his rescue mission, Lieut. Clarke had become the target for every Indian rifle and how he was able to accomplish his heroic feat unscathed is a miracle, for not a single Indian bullet touched him. The wounded trooper was gently laid behind a rock safe from further harm.

Lieut. Clarke's citation reads: "rushed forward to the rescue of a soldier who was severely wounded and lay disabled, exposed to the enemy's fire and carried him to a place of safety."

Ten days later, on 15 May, a hostile Apache camp situated between the Santa Cruz and San Pedro Rivers, was located. A spirited charge managed to win the Indian village, but when the troops attempted to make their way back to camp, they were ambushed by the Apaches in a box canyon. After killing two troopers and wounding two more, the Indians withdrew.

KNIGHTS WITHOUT ARMOR

There may be some people who think patriotism is old-fashioned. There may be some people who think decorations are nothing more than gaudy strips of ribbon or odd-shaped pieces of metal surrounded by hollow ceremonies. Perhaps to some, the Medal of Honor is a gaudy strip of ribbon and an odd-shaped piece of metal, but those who won them on the fields of battle for outstanding acts of valor, know the price paid in blood, agony and sacrifice.

The sanguinary battle at Wounded Knee Creek, South Dakota, on 29 December 1890, was one of the last armed clashes between the American Indian and the cavalry trooper. It marked the beginning of the end to a violent era. This battle, on a bleak and barren Dakota plain, lasted less than an hour, yet it was as desperate an encounter as combat can be. The Indians called it the Messiah War while the whites dubbed it the Messiah Craze.

The Sioux Indians were one of the largest and most prosperous of the plains Indian tribes. They had always led a wild and proud existence prior to the coming of the white man. They had roamed the vast ranges of their wild and untamed lands, at will. They had existed solely upon the wild game so bountiful in the Dakotas.

According to the treaty of 1868, all of South Dakota was to belong to the Sioux: ". . . for as long as the grass shall grow and the sun shall shine . . ." In 1874, a military expedi-

161

tion was sent into the sacred Black Hills. When it was reported that ". . . gold could be found clinging to the roots of the grass . . ." white settlers and gold seekers began to inundate the Black Hills in search of the "yellow iron."

While all of this was taking place, the white "buffalo hunters," continued to systematically destroy the Indian's natural commissary.

By the end of the year 1875, Indian depredations had become so fierce, relations between the red man and the white man had been strained to the breaking point. Political pressures compelled the War Department to issue a directive stating ". . . that all Indians not on reservations by the end of 31 January next, shall be treated as being hostile by the military forces then on the frontier . . ."

Following the legendary battle of the Little Big Horn River in 1876, the old mode of living for the Sioux was no more. They were forced to relinquish one third of their reservation lands, which included the Black Hills. Their unbridled freedom to roam at will was now only a glorious memory.

In the past, the Sioux had been able to depend solely upon the buffalo to supply them with the necessities of life. By 1884, the buffalo were virtually non-existent on the vast Dakota plains and the nomadic Sioux were forced to take up the tools of the farmer in order to survive.

From 1886 to 1890, diseases made serious inroads to the Indian cattle herds. Crop failure upon crop failure found them in dire straits. Epidemics of measles, whooping cough and influenza swept through the Indian camps like a prairie fire, exacting a terrible toll.

On 1 January 1889, while a total eclipse of the sun was in progress, a Piute Indian in Nevada, named Wovoka, reportedly fell into a trance and was informed by the Great Spirit that he had been chosen to lead his people out of bondage. According to this new Messiah, the end of the Indian dilemma was now in sight. Come the spring of 1891, God would appear to rid the Indian lands of all whites and restore a regenerated soil to its rightful heirs.

The Ghost Dances being performed by the Indians alarmed the whites. The Indians were ordered to cease such dances at once. The Indians refused. They began to gather in large concentrations to perform their Ghost Dances.

The white settlers called upon the War Department for help.

General Nelson A. Miles, now commander of the Military Department of the Missouri, was placed in charge of the troops whose orders were to protect the white settlers at all costs and, if possible, try to prevent a serious outbreak among the Sioux. Approximately 3,000 troops were moved into the Black Hills and stationed at strategic locations throughout the threatened area.

By November of 1890, the heavy concentrations of troops now began to frighten the Indians camped near the Pine Ridge Agency. They began an exodus into the natural fortified areas of the Badlands to continue their Ghost Dancing. Meanwhile, those Indians from the Rosebud and Pine Ridge Agencies already in the Badlands were surrounded by General Miles' troops. A parley with the Indians was arranged. After repeated assurances of fair treatment, the Ghost Dancers capitulated. On 27 December, the Sioux, now numbering upwards of 3,000 braves, were escorted back to the Pine Ridge Agency.

However, peace was not to be at this time. That same day, word was received that a large band of Sioux had evaded the troopers and made good their escape. Three troops of cavalry were, at once, ordered into the field to try and intercept the runaways. The troops were first ordered to scout about eighteen miles from the Agency and then bivouac for the night along the banks of Wounded Knee Creek.

During the darkened hours, an exceptionally heavy snowfall covered the ground with a thick blanket of white. The icy winds, spawned somewhere in the frigid Arctic, chilled everyone to the bone. Animals and men alike suffered greatly from the bitter cold which registered well below zero.

Next morning, scouts from the camp at Wounded Knee Creek were sent out in an attempt to locate the wayward In-

163

dians. They were quickly located about nine miles away on the banks of Porcupine Creek. Heavy columns were hurridly dispatched and the Indians quickly surrounded. The troopers ordered the Indians to surrender. Once again, the Indians, so surprised by the movements of the troopers in such bitterly cold weather, surrendered meekly and returned to the army camp at Wounded Knee Creek. The ranks of the troops at Wounded Knee Creek had, by now, been reinforced to total almost 480 soldiers. Both camps were astir at dawn on 29 December.

The military had taken every precautionary measure possible to discourage any rash attempts on the part of the Sioux. The Indians were camped on a flat open plain in front of a dry ravine. A white flag of truce was emplanted in the ground next to the tent of the chief. Seventy-six dismounted troopers encircled the entire encampment as sentinels. A company of mounted Indian scouts was lined up on the south bank of the dry ravine which was adjacent to the Indians' camp. These, in turn, were backed up by two troops of mounted cavalry. One troop of mounted cavalry flanked the east side of the Indian camp, while another troop of mounted cavalry was stationed on the northwest side. A battery of Hotchkiss guns was positioned on a mound overlooking the entire scene. Two troops of cavalry were dismounted and stood guard near the chief's teepee.

Upon completion of the disposition of the troops, the Indians were ordered from their teepees. Wrapped in blankets to protect themselves from the cruel wind, the braves moved sullenly forward and squatted in a semi-circle in the snow.

An interpreter informed them, they must surrender their firearms.

The Indians were far from pleased. They argued vehemently about the necessity of retaining their old fowling pieces to kill game. Their pleas fell on deaf ears. They were ordered to return to their teepees and surrender their weapons.

After considerable debate amongst themselves, several scowling braves moved toward their tents, returning with two old muzzle-loading weapons, declaring the two old relics to be the only weapons in their possession. This ruse also fell upon deaf ears. The troops were ordered to begin a search of the teepees and confiscate any weapons located. At first the Sioux braves became agitated, which quickly turned to irritation, by the wails of the squaws who were attempting to prevent the soldiers from scattering their belongings in their search for weapons. Tensions rose.

In his native tongue, the medicine man began exhorting his people to resist the blue-coats. Then as the soldiers stepped forward to search the blanketed warriors, the medicine man stopped his prancing, stooped over, scooped a handful of dirt and flung it into the air. This was the traditional Indian summons to battle. One of the troopers flipped back, a blanket covering one of the braves, revealing a modern rifle, cocked and loaded. In the struggle for the possession of the weapon, the gun discharged. The shot was like the dropping of a match into an open keg of gunpowder. The whole field exploded into action.

The troopers, oblivious to anything but self-preservation, began firing into the erupting mass of Indians. The Sioux warriors threw off their blankets to reveal the weapons the soldiers had been seeking and began to return the troopers' fire at point-blank range. Those Indians who did not possess firearms, savagely attacked the soldiers with hatchet, knife, and war-club. The white-hot fury of this mad melee almost defies description. The air was rent by savage war cries and booming of guns.

The rifle fire of the troopers, at once, became as deadly to themselves as it did to the Indians. The troopers flanking the camp began to fire their carbines wildly into the seething mass of humanity, subjecting everyone within the circle to a deadly crossfire. Volleys of hot lead from the Hotchkiss guns commanding the scene, mowed down individuals, both trooper and Indian alike, in droves.

In the midst of all this bedlam, many Indians began to take up positions in their teepees, delivering a murderous vol-

165

ley of fire as sharpshooters. The bulk of the Indians, however, were fleeing helter-skelter for the sanctuary of the dry ravine, in an effort to escape the horrendous volley of fire being delivered by the troopers. When the Hotchkiss battery saw what the Indians were endeavoring to do, they quickly repositioned their field pieces to deliver an enfilade fire into the dry ravine, and the Indians who had sought shelter there, were literaly cut to ribbons by a relentless storm of lead. Other Indians attempting to flee across the open plain in stark terror were ridden down by the troopers. The troopers showed little mercy. Few, if any, of the fleeing Indians escaped their pent-up wrath and frustration.

As suddenly as it had started, the firing stopped. Dead Indians lay strewn about the plains as far as the eye could see. The moans and piteous cries of the wounded and dying filled the air.

Eighteen men were awarded Medals of Honor for this brief, but deadly clash, with the troublesome Sioux. An example of the savagery of the battle was that of Captain Wallace, the only officer killed on that day. Captain Wallace had four bullet wounds on his body, but actually succumbed to a blow on the head delivered by an Indian warclub.

Sergeants William G. Austin and Albert W. McMillan, "while engaged with Indians concealed in a ravine, assisted the men on the skirmish line, directed their fire, encouraged them, by example, and used every effort to dislodge the enemy."

Musician John E. Clancy "twice voluntarily exposed himself to the fire of the Indians when he dashed out onto the open plain to rescue comrades who had been wounded and were lying on the field of battle exposed to further hazards."

First Lieutenant Earnest A. Garlington "voluntarily led a detail of soldiers into a ravine in an attempt to dislodge Indians concealed therein."

Private Joshua B. Hartzog "voluntarily went to the rescue of his commanding officer, who had fallen severely wounded from the Indian fire, picked him up and carried him out of range of the hostiles guns.''

Also awarded Medals were Private Mosheim Feaster; First Lieutenant John C. Gresham; Private Mathew H. Hamilton; Second Lieutenant Harry L. Hawthorne; Private Marvin C. Hillock; Private George Hobday; Sergeant George Loyd; Private Thomas Sullivan; First Sergeant Frederick E. Toy; First Sergeant Jacob Trautman; Corporal Paul H. Weinert; Sergeant James Ward; and Private Hermann Ziegner.

The reverberating thunder of the battle was heard by the Indians congregated at the Agency, and when stragglers of the battle began to appear and report the affair, the Sioux camp was thrown into a turmoil. Many of the now panic-stricken Indians took this as an omen that the soldiers intended to kill them all. As a result, many of the warriors headed for the battlefield, bent on avenging the dead.

In the meantime, the troops were still on the battlefield hunting stragglers and gathering up the dead, when this new band of Sioux warriors appeared on the horizon. Once again, the Indians and soldiers engaged in deadly combat. The troopers quickly threw up a set of breastworks and managed to repel the Indian assaults. A runner brought word to the troops in the field that the Agency was also under attack by Indians. A detachment of troopers was hastily dispatched to bolster the besieged post. As the troopers approached the Agency, those Indians withdrew to a position on White Clay Creek.

Even though the entire complement of troopers was back at the Agency, the next day, the situation still was not solved. The troopers were outnumbered at least three to one by the now thoroughly riled Sioux. Two more battles were fought with the Sioux along the White Clay Creek and White River, before a blizzard blew up and smothered the Dakotas and any further battles beneath a blanket of snow. Thus did the Indian campaigns come to an official end.

Medals awarded for actions at White Clay Creek, 30 December 1890, and White River, 1 January 1891, include Corporal William V. Wilson; Sergeant Bernhard Jetter; Corporal

Adam Neder; Farrier Richard J. Nolan; First Sergeant Theodore Ragnar; Captain Charles A. Varnum; Captain John B. Kerr; Sergeant Joseph F. Knight; Sergeant Fred Meyers; First Lieutenant Benjamin H. Cheever, Jr.; Second Lieutenant Robert L. Howze; and Corporal Cornelius C. Smith.

SOME OTHERS WHO ALSO SERVED

George E. Albee, First Lieutenant, 41st U.S. Infantry, at Brazos River, Texas, "attacked with two men a force of eleven Indians, drove them from the hills, and reconnoitered the country beyond."

John B. Babcock, First Lieutenant, 5th U.S. Cavalry, at Spring Creek, Nebraska, "while serving with a scouting column, this officer's troop was attacked by a vastly superior force of Indians. Advancing to high ground, he dismounted his men, remaining mounted himself to encourage them, and there fought the Indians until relieved, his horse being wounded."

Charles A. Bessy, Corporal, 3rd U.S. Cavalry, near Elkhorn Creek, Wyoming, "while scouting with four men and attacked in ambush by fourteen hostile Indians, held his ground, two of his men being wounded, and kept up the fight until himself wounded in the side, and then went to the assistance of his wounded comrades."

William C. Bryan, Hospital Steward, U.S. Army, at Powder River, Wyoming, "accompanied a detachment of cavalry in a charge on a village of hostile Indians and fought through the engagements, having his horse killed under him. He continued to fight on foot, and under severe fire and without assistance conveyed two wounded comrades to places of safety, saving them from capture."

Matthias W. Day, Second Lieutenant, 9th U.S. Cavalry, at Las Animas Canyon, New Mexico, "advanced alone into

169

the enemy's lines and carried off a wounded soldier of his command under a hot fire and after he had been ordered to retreat.''

Francis S. Dodge, Captain, 8th U.S. Cavalry, near White River Agency, Colorado, ''with a force of forty men rode all night to the relief of a command that had been defeated and was besieged by an overwhelming force of Indians, reached the field at daylight, joined in the action and fought for 3 days.''

James Fegan, Sergeant, 3rd U.S. Infantry, at Plum Creek, Kansas, ''while in charge of a powder train enroute from Fort Harker to Fort Dodge, Kansas, was attacked by a party of desperadoes, who attempted to rescue a deserter in his charge and to fire the train. Sergeant Fegan, single-handed, repelled the attacking party, wounding two of them and brought his train through in safety.''

Michael Glynn, Private, 5th U.S. Cavalry, at Whetstone Mountains, Arizona, ''drove off, single-handed, eight hostile Indians, killing and wounding five.''

George Grant, Sergeant, 18th U.S. Infantry, at Fort Philadelphia Kearney to Fort C. F. Smith, Dakota Territory, ''bravery, energy and perseverance, involving much suffering and privation through attacks by hostile Indians, deep snows, etc., while voluntarily carrying dispatches.''

Private George Hooker, 1st U.S. Cavalry, at Tonto Creek, Arizona, ''gallantry in action in which he was killed.''

Leonard Wood, Assistant Surgeon, U.S. Army, in Apache campaigns, summer of 1886, ''voluntarily carried dispatches through a region infested with hostile Indians, making a journey of 70 miles in one night and walking 30 miles the next day. Also, for several weeks, while in close pursuit of Geronimo's band and constantly expecting an encounter, commanded a detachment of infantry, which was then without an officer, and to the command of which he was assigned upon his own request.''

THE LAST HERO

Officially, as far as the Army was concerned, the Indian campaigns had been closed for some time, in fact, since 30 December 1891. But now, on a small point of land called Sugar Point, in Leech Lake Minnesota, the American trooper harkened to "Boots and Saddles" for one last fight with the Indians of North America. There was to be one last Medal of Honor awarded for the Indian campaigns and it came during an uprising of the Chippewa Indians on 5 October 1898.

The Chippewas' homeland was located in northern Minnesota and they had always been peaceful toward the white man. At Leech Lake, they staged their first and only uprising.

In 1898, several hundred Chippewas lived on Bear Island, a small piece of land less than two miles wide by four miles long which lay about three miles off the eastern shore of Leech Lake.

Sometime in April 1895, the leader of this group had been arrested for giving whiskey to another Indian. When the only witness to the transaction conveniently disappeared, the leader was released, but was later subpoenaed by the same court the following June, this time as a witness.

Ignoring the summons, the leader was arrested for contempt of court. Confined in jail, he was summarily freed by a small group of loyal tribesmen. Warrants were immediately issued for the chief and twelve of his followers.

171

Through indifference on the part of some of the whites, the Indians were not brought to face the court until May of 1897, and then only nine appeared. The Indians pleaded guilty to the charges and were sentenced to thirty days in jail. The leader of this group was not one of the nine to be sentenced and little effort was made to bring him in until September of 1898. Plans had been made to serve the warrant in his name when he appeared to collect his next annuity check.

Everything went according to plan and then the leader was once more freed by his followers. The U.S. marshal at St. Paul, Minnesota, immediately secured warrants for the apprehension and arrest of twenty-two Indians, all part of the liberating party, and requested a squad of troopers be assigned to assist him.

The War Department, atonce, sent twenty troopers from Fort Snelling, under the command of Lieutenant C. B. Humphries, to assist the Federal officer. When Lieut. Humphries heard rumors that the Chippewas planned to resist, he telegraphed for reinforcements.

On 3 October, a council between the Indian agent, the Indian inspector, and the Indians, bore little fruit as far as getting the Indians to relenquish the guilty parties. The following day, eighty troopers arrived in Walker, five miles from the Agency. The same day a peace mission between the Federal marshal, the Indian inspector and the Indians, this time held on Sugar Point, also failed.

On 5 October, two lake steamers, one towing a barge loaded with thirty troopers, made the thirty mile run up Leech Lake from Walker to Sugar Point. Upon their arrival at Sugar Point, the troopers found it almost deserted but did manage to capture one of the fugitives they sought.

After a hasty reconnaissance of the area, the troops began to prepare for noon chow. While the troops were stacking arms, one of the pieces was accidentally discharged.

Indian snipers had concealed themselves in the woods surrounding the Army camp and this accidental firing precipitated a vicious volley of rifle fire from them. One soldier was killed

172

instantly and several others seriously wounded. The troopers immediately recovered and formed a skirmish line. A hot exchange of rifle and carbine fire ensued, which lasted more than a half an hour.

Sniping continued the rest of the day with two more soldiers being fatally struck by Indian fire. As darkness began to limit visibility, the troopers set about constructing breastworks and rifle pits and posting sentries in anticipation of an Indian attack they were sure would come with the first light of the next day.

The Chippewas, however, settled down to the same sniping tactics which had stood them in such good stead the day before. Several more troopers were wounded in addition to the Indian inspector and the U.S. marshal. One of the Indian policemen assigned to the troops was mistakenly shot by one of the soldiers who thought the Indian to be a Chippewa.

Realizing the futility of trying to ferret out the Chippewas from behind their concealment in the dense woods, the troops executed an orderly withdrawal from Sugar Point on 7 October.

Expecting a general uprising, the War Department quickly sent two hundred additional troops from Fort Snelling to bolster those already at the Agency. One hundred additional men were assigned to guard the dams in the Leech Lake vicinity. Two batteries of National Guard Artillery and several companies of Minnesota Infantry were called to active duty. The thirty-five Indians now completely surrounded on Bear Island had no intention of starting anything.

The Commissioner of U.S. Indian Affairs arrived at the Agency on 10 October. At the same time, a priest from the local mission, also arrived. Because the Padre was well liked by the Indians, he was given a canoe loaded with trade goods and sent to arrange a council with the Indians.

On 12 October, the Indians met with the Commissioner on Indian Affairs, who demanded the surrender of those on the warrants. The Indians refused unless some promise of immunity was given. When the Commissioner saw signs of ending

173

the rebellion if certain situations could be stabilized, the Indians were given a chance to air their grievances. The Indians then promised not to engage in any more hostilities, and then threw themselves on the mercy of the Great White Father.

By 20 October, most of the Indians on the warrants were in custody except the leader who was still at large. The prisoners were taken to Duluth, Minnesota, where fines and jail sentences were meted out. However, the Commissioner on Indian Affairs, feeling the punishment was much too severe, had the fines returned and the jail sentence reduced to two months. On 3 January 1899, President McKinley issued full pardons to all Indians involved in the uprising.

Private Oscar Burkhard, Hospital Corps, U.S. Army, "bravery in action against hostile Indians, 5 October 1898."

* * *

Thus did the Indian war drums cease to throb. Thus did nearly three decades of unrest come to peace. The Indian had fought well and at times, had proven superior. But in the long run, he could not compete with the white man's weapons and the superior fighting qualities of the American soldier.

The Indian began to accept the white man's ways and pick up the tools of the farmer. To many, the inner fires never ceased to burn.

With the war drums stilled, the American trooper began to fade into the past. Gone was the excitement of the charge. Gone were the days in the saddle on some hard campaign. Next was to come the tank. and the plane. The American trooper would have to go unto the breech against the hostile Indians no more.